Retiring to Our Garden
Year Two - 2nd Edition

Retiring to Our Garden - Year Two - 2nd Edition is the continuing story of the development of our Norfolk garden. It is told in words covering a year in our garden from May 2014 to April 2015 and in pictures of our garden over a six year period from May 2014 to July 2019. The idea is to tell the story of the changes in the life of our garden over time!

by Norfolk Watercolour Artist - Alan R .Massen
Published in Great Britain by Rainbow Publications UK

First Published in 2015 by Rainbow Publications UK
2nd Edition Published in 2019 by Rainbow Publications UK

Copyright © 2019 Alan R. Massen

The moral right of Alan R. Massen to be identified as the author of this work has been asserted in accordance with the UK Copyright, Designs and Patents Act of 1988.

All rights reserved.

No part of this book may be reproduced, or stored in a retrieval system, or transmitted in any form or by any means, electronic, mechanical, photocopying, recording, or otherwise, without the prior written permission of both the author and the above publisher of this book
All imagery and illustrations © Alan R. Massen

Neither the publisher nor the author can accept liability for the use of any of the materials, methods or information recommended in this book or for any consequences arising out of their use, nor can they be held responsible for any errors or omissions that may be found in the text or may occur at a future date as a result of changes in rules, laws or equipment

All manufacturers, sellers, product names and services identified in this book are used in editorial fashion and for the benefit of such companies with no intention of any infringement of trademarks. No such use or the use of any trade name is intended to convey endorsement or other affiliation with this book

Paperback Edition ISBN: 978-0-9933962-0-5

Published in Great Britain by Rainbow Publications UK
Typeset in Minion Pro

About the Author

Alan was born in the city of Norwich in the county of Norfolk, England in November 1949. When Alan was still a teenager he started painting whilst attending art classes in Norwich. In his mid-teens he had two paintings accepted for a National Art Exhibition held in London and other major UK cities. Alan spent most of his working life as a professional Health and Safety Advisor and rarely picked up a paint brush until he, his wife Susie and daughter Ginny (his other daughter Mandy is married and lives with her husband Adrian in Sheffield) moved out of the city of Norwich into the countryside in 1993. They moved to a little village called East Lexham in the heart of Norfolk. The village was very peaceful and pretty. This helped inspire Alan to take up watercolour painting once again. In 2004 they moved to another small West Norfolk village near Downham Market where they still live today. In 2008 Alan had to retire due to ill health (bad knees). He continued to paint in watercolours regularly and also started writing. He has had forty six books published to-date. In 2019 he produced this Book that showcases Norfolk the County of his birth.

Dedication

I would like to dedicate this book, to our daughters Mandy and Ginny. I would also like to acknowledge our friends Andy, Lynn, Corri, Alistair, Issy, Karl, Anna and all our Greek friends at the Troulos Bay Hotel and at the Mythos Cafe on the Greek Paradise Island of Skiathos for all their friendship over the many years we have visited there. A very special thank you must go to my wife Susie who helps and supports me everyday of my life. I love you to the moon and back!

Books by the Author

- Retiring to our Garden Year One   - Retiring to our Garden Year Two
- Retiring into a Rainbow   - Retiring into a Rainbow 2nd Edition
- Skiathos a Greek Island Paradise   - Norfolk the County of my Birth 2nd Edition
- Art Inspired by a Rainbow   - Ibiza Island of Dreams
- Majorca Island in the Sun   - Flip-Flops and Shades on Thassos
- Mardle and a Troshin' in Norfolk   - England the Country of my Birth
- Mousehole the Cornish Jewel   - Sunshades and Flip-Flops on Kefalonia
- Shades and Flip-Flops on Zakynthos   - Trips into my Mind's Eye 2nd Edition
- Corfu and Mainland Greece   - Crete and the Island of Santorini
- Cyprus, the Pyramids and the Holy Land - Greek Islands in the Sun
- Trips into My Mind's Eye   - Norfolk the County of my Birth
- Being Greek "The Culture of the People of Greece"

Copyright © 2019 Alan R. Massen
I hope you enjoy this my latest book featuring Our Norfolk Garden

Books by the Author

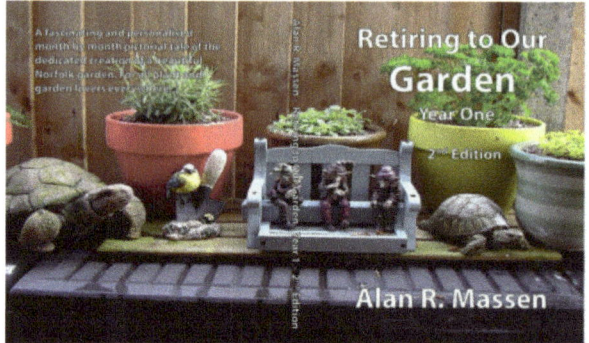

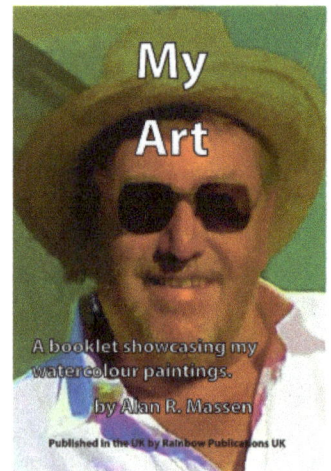
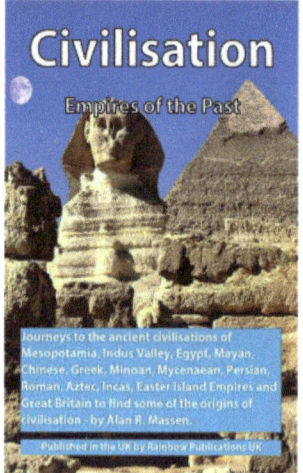

Books and Booklets by Alan R. Massen

Books by the Author

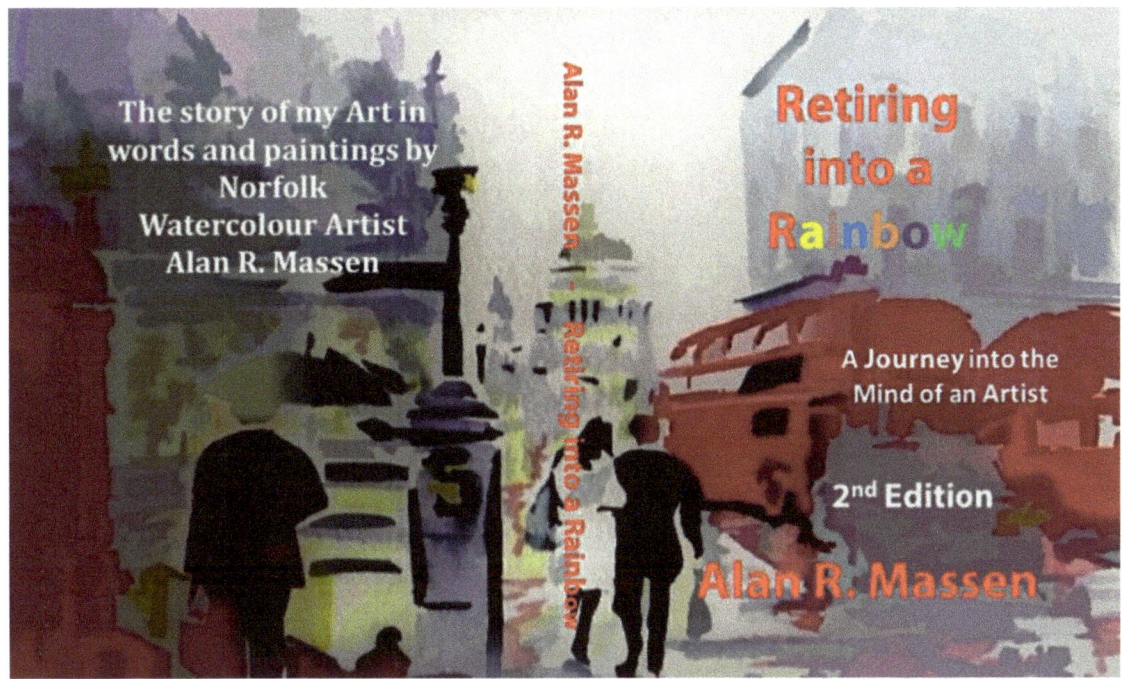

Books and Booklets by Alan R. Massen

Books by the Author

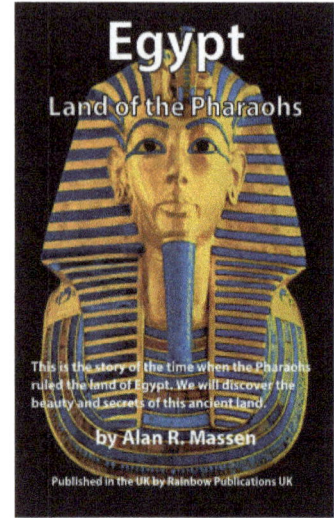
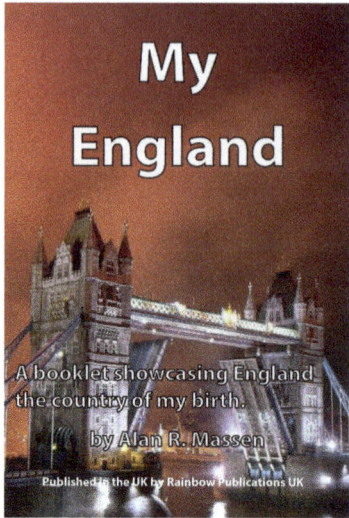
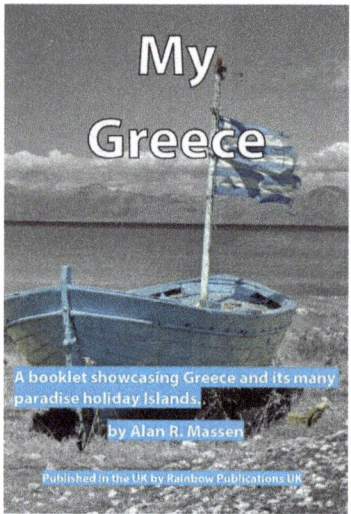

Books and Booklets by Alan R. Massen

Books by the Author

Books and Booklets by Alan R. Massen

Books by the Author

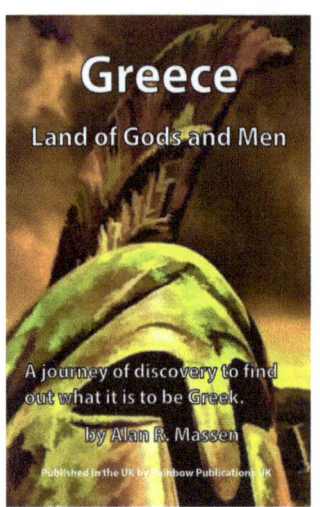
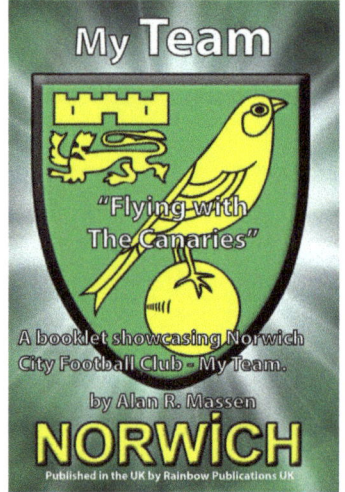
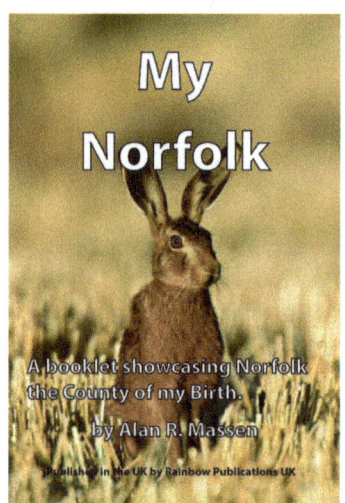

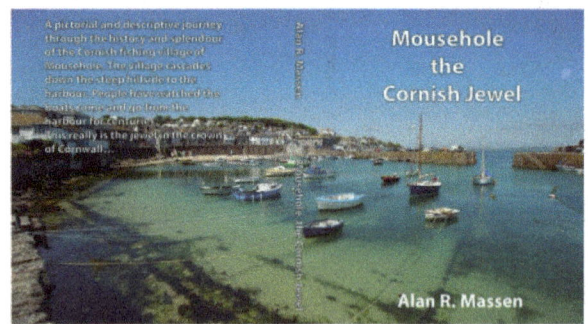

Books and Booklets by Alan R. Massen

Books by the Author

Books and Booklets by Alan R. Massen

Books by the Author

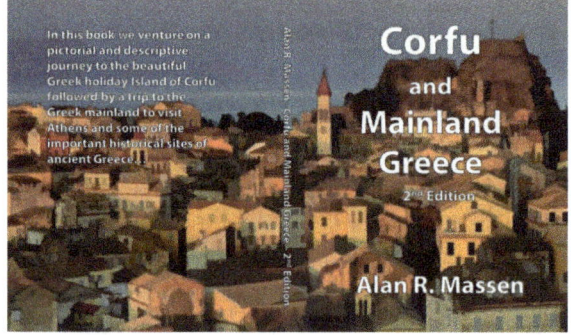

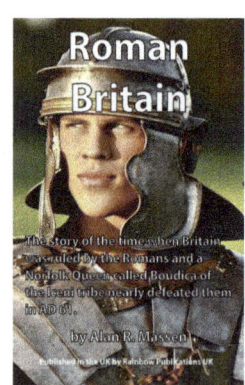

Books and Booklets by Alan R. Massen

Books by the Author

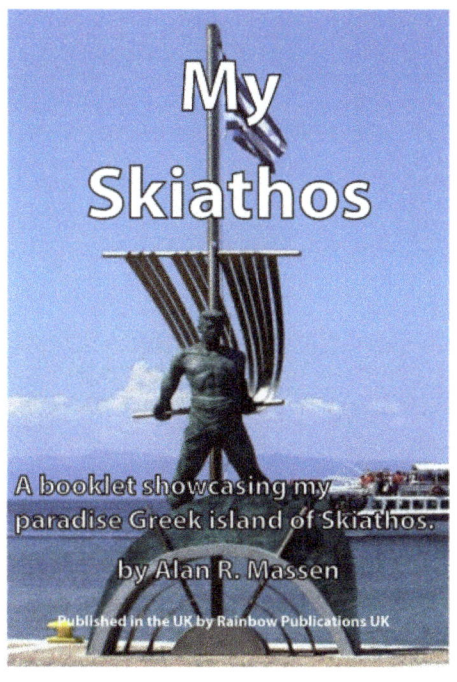

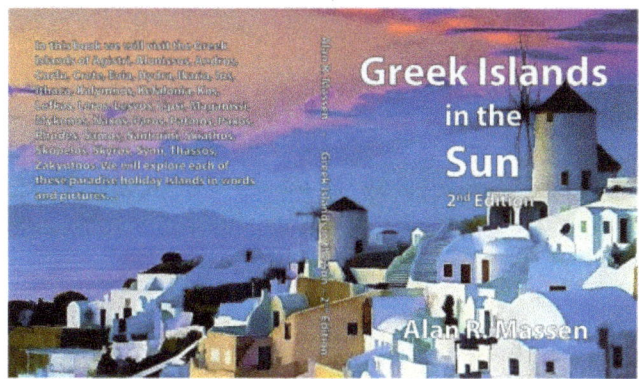
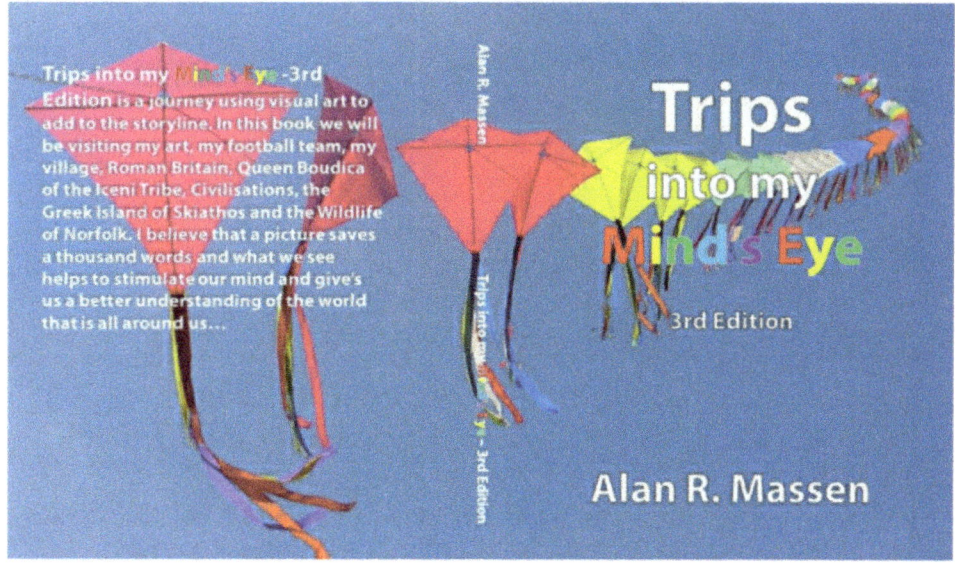

Books and Booklets by Alan R. Massen

Contents

Introduction	1
April 2014	4
May 2014	14
June 2014	58
July 2014	103
August 2014	131
September 2014	145
October 2014	169
November 2014	189
December 2014	199
January 2015	203
February 2015	210
March 2015	223
April 2015	238
The Prologue from 2016 to 2019	262
Acknowledgement	286

Copyright © 2019 Alan R. Massen

Introduction

Let us start at the very beginning!

This is my second book in the series: **"Retiring to our Garden - Year Two"** and follows on from where the previous book finished so I would recommend that you read **"Retiring to the garden - Year One"** before going any further! All my books are available on line on Amazon and other good book retailers! Now that I have completed my promotional sales pitch and to ensure continuity I think it is well worth revisiting my introduction used in my first book.

The story so far!

Having recently retired from a hectic professional job I was now entering a new phase of my life called retirement. This meant that I now had the time to spend on my two hobbies of watercolour painting and gardening. Little did I know at the time that these activities would take up so much of my waking hours? To help me maximise my efforts my wife Susie bought me some watercolour paint, paper pads, brushes and a greenhouse. The first step was to make a plan of how I was going to divide my effort between painting and gardening. Luckily Mother Nature largely decided this for me as even to me it was obvious that certain times of the year were conducive to outdoor activities (i.e. Spring and Summer) like gardening and at other times (i.e. autumn and winter) would be better spent inside painting. So I decided to largely garden between April and September and paint between October and March...

Introduction

The studio!

To this end I appropriated our dining room table as my art studio (much to Susie's dismay) and a cupboard in the kitchen to keep my planting kit (dibber and plant tags) along with my many tins and packets of seeds (also bought by Susie). I realised very quickly that this plan would need to be flexible because sometimes I would want to paint in the garden in the summer or pot up seeds indoors (and propagate on our spare bedroom window sill, much to Susie's consternation) in the months of January and February. I had already taken cuttings of fuchsias, sages and other plants to over winter in our sun lounge last year. Susie took this intrusion into one of our main downstairs room well and some may argue that this was at least some of her motivation in buying me a greenhouse. However, this plan if that is what she had in mind, may not have worked out as she hoped! So I had a plan and now it was time to put it into action. Susie also encouraged me to keep a diary so I could learn from my successes and also my failures!

Back to the future!

I started my note taking on the 25th April 2014 and wrote on the front page: **The Massen Garden ... "A second year in the life of our Garden"**... with a main title of: "Retiring to our Garden" Year TWO". So the year began. Most days, or when something special or notable happened, I wrote it down in my diary. One year on and I had not only filled up three notebooks with information, some of which was even interesting but I now found that I enjoyed the act of writing my ramblings down so much that now I had a third hobby, one of writing! I had also found time to produce artworks of our garden and landscapes, portraits of people, animals and other interesting things. It was always my intention to write a follow up book which would again include my observations and artwork so as to produce a continuing series of books. This offering is called: **"Retiring to our Garden – Year TWO - a further year in the life of our garden"**...

Introduction

The use of modern technology!

You will notice throughout my journal, that some of my pictures look out of focus! These are not due to my standard of photography, but are the products of my excitement at discovering some art software on my PC that give an impressionist effect… a bit like Monet! I recommend that you get yourself some hobbies: I believe that when you retire you must have some hobbies and pastimes that keep your mind and body active but remember that like the Greeks you need some relaxation time for coffee/tea and reflection.

So armed with a trowel, plants, seeds, pencil and notebook:

LET'S GO GARDENING!

After the above pictures of Susie and me we are at last ready to venture out into our garden to begin another exciting year in the life of our garden. I hope you enjoy my latest offering…

April 2014 in our Garden

In the beginning (Day One – Year Two)!

Friday 25th April: Typical of the UK weather my first day of the new season and it rained all day. Still it is April after all and this month is famous for April showers! Being stuck indoors I used my time wisely by completing my first book of last years gardening exploits:

Front garden stepped terrace bed completed in May 2019…

This done I decided to use the rest of the day making a check list of all the things I need to do over the next few weeks in the garden. It is always surprising just how many things need to be done when you write them down in black and white. I filled a whole sheet of A 4 paper and sat back thinking help am I ever going to get all this work done…

April 2014 in our Garden

Things to do

- Completely empty out the greenhouse of pots, trough and staging
- Remove the bubble wrap used in the greenhouse over winter to keep it warmer
- Once the glass is cleaned return the trough, staging and pots back into the greenhouse
- Fill the trough with compost. fertilizer and water retention gel ready for planting up with the plants that I have grown from seed
- Move tomatoes, cucumber and sweet pepper plants from the sun lounge and plant into the prepared pots in the greenhouse
- Plant out all of the plants grown from cuttings, seeds and plug plants that had been kept in the greenhouse away from any frosts into the borders, baskets and pots
- Plant up the front garden pots and borders with any spare plants left over after planting up the back garden beds and pots
- Top dress all of the pots front and back with horticultural grit once planted up to help retain moisture and suppress weeds
- Visit garden centres and nurseries to buy additional plants to fill any spaces left after planting out the plants from the greenhouse
- Treat shed and seat with wood preserver using the same colour (willow) as they are currently treated with
- Fix windbreak material (already bought) in two of the arches of the smoke room (car port)
- Weed front drive with hoe and/or weed killer and then rake the surface level once more
- Feed all newly planted plants as soon as possible after planting and repeat every two to three weeks thereafter
- Mow front bank and back lawn, feed birds, water, feed plants and dead head flowers as and when required

A visitor to our garden…

Better get ready…

April 2014 in our Garden

The postman and Susie come bearing gifts!

Today also saw the arrival by post of the six plug plants that we ordered some weeks ago. These are climbing plants called "Lofos – Burgundy Falls". The climbing/tumbling plugs I potted up into one litre pots and put them into the greenhouse to grow on before I plant them out later.

What a surprise!

Susie arrived home from work bearing a gift… She had bought me a "Dentata Lavender Tree". We will need to get a large pot to plant it in before putting it on the decking for summer display.

The big boy is back!

Saturday 26th April: This morning our old friend the pheasant returned to our garden. We call him Oliver because he always asks for more! We had not seen him since we returned from our Easter break in Sheffield so it was a relief when he reappeared for his breakfast…

April 2014 in our Garden

Just popping out!

Today was again cold 11°C and wet so I popped out to the shops to get a large plant pot so I could pot up the lavender tree Susie brought home yesterday. It looks great on the decking in its pot in the back middle of the decking.

The decking that we made at the top of our garden

April 2014 in our Garden

My bleeding heart!

The good thing about all this rain is that the bleeding heart in our right hand side back garden bed is looking very good and full of blooms.

One of the clematis planted last year is now in full bloom and making a valiant attempt at covering the murdered hedge…

April 2014 in our Garden

Down with the bubble!

Sunday 27th April: This morning Susie and I decided to empty the greenhouse and take down the bubble wrap that we used to keep the greenhouse snug and warm all winter:

The greenhouse looked great and with everything put back in (minus the bubble wrap of course) and the Lime and Lemon trees back guarding either side of the greenhouse door all was ready for this new year in our greenhouse! This done we lined the trough with lining material then filled it with compost, water gel and fertilizer. We also returned the staging, fruit pots for the tomatoes, cucumber and sweet peppers and more than three hundred one litre pots of the plants that we have grown from cuttings, seeds and plug plants. The plants we are currently growing on in the greenhouse before planting them outside as soon as the weather improves. This accomplished we retired to the decking for drinks and a sit in the welcome sun that has now reappeared at last…

April 2014 in our Garden

Fuchsias galore!

Monday 28th April: This morning I decided to plant up all of the pre-prepared plant pots in the front garden with twelve of the fuchsias that I have grown from cuttings. This left just ten pots in the front garden without any plants in so gathering more plants from the greenhouse I planted these up with Dahlias, Delphinium Fox, Nemesia Royal Ensign and fuchsia Thalia. This completed I top dressed all of the planted up front pots with horticultural grit and gave them a good watering. Then it was on to the greenhouse to water all the pots of plants and then outside to feed the birds before taking our cat Marble to the vets because he had not eaten for three days and was not very well…

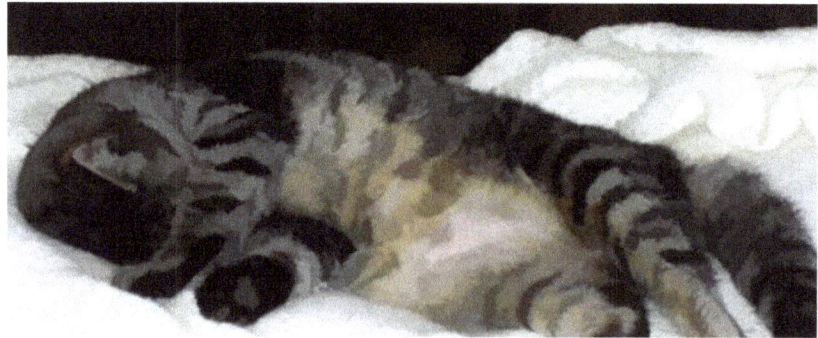

Marble feeling poorly!

The vet said that she thought he had eaten something he should not have done (no change there then) so she gave him an injection and special food that we have to syringe into him for the next three days. After that he should be ok…

April 2014 in our Garden

More shopping!

Tuesday 29th April: Today we went out in the morning to get a large bag of wild bird seed and some peanuts from a shop called Beart's because the birds have nearly finished what we have. Whilst out we also went to the obligatory garden centre this time the Downham Country Store and came away with a new seed tray for the birds, a bag of rose, tree and shrub compost and two bags of horticultural grit as we are running low on both compost and grit. We also purchased a new clematis plant called Mme Baron Velliard to grow up the palm plant that has lost all of its leaves:

The palm lost its leaves when I brought it out of the sun lounge to early and Jack Frost got it! But it stills makes a two metre high sculptural addition to our garden! When the clematis climbs up its five stems it should look great…

April 2014 in our Garden

Putting the Black with Blue lights all over!

In the afternoon Susie removed the blue solar lights that she had put temporarily on the palm stems so I could plant the new clematis ready to train it up the stems as it grows. She then put the blue solar lights into the black elder bush further up the bed near the silver birch tree. So we will now be able to see the lights at night from our kitchen window as well as from the patio. Talking of the patio our new stump holding the water pump is looking good and the ivy Susie planted in it is growing well:

Out with the Old and in with the New!

There is a certain charm in seeing, side by side, the old way that you would get water e.g. The water pump against the new way of getting water the plastic hosepipe seen attached to the outside water tap. They say that life moves on and thankfully this is true for gardeners who need an easy and convenient water supply for their garden and sometimes changes over time can make life easier and even improve our lot in life…

April 2014 in our Garden

News flash!

Wednesday 30th April: This morning I sowed six one litre pots with marigold seeds and put them into the greenhouse to germinate.

Marigolds in our garden

I heard on Gardeners Question Time on BBC Four on Sunday that if you plant marigolds near tomatoes it helps prevent white fly. As I am always ready to try new things I will do the same when I plant my tomatoes into pots in the greenhouse this year. This programme and the one on BBC Radio Norfolk on a Saturday afternoon called The Garden Party has given me some great tips over the years such as. Not pruning back your plants until early spring, feed each new plant that you plant with a dressing of blood, fish and bone fertilizer at the roots and using evergreen clematis to help hide a murdered hedge! I imagine that planting marigolds next to tomatoes will also prove successful too…

May 2014 in our Garden

Boxes of pure colour!

The postman delivered this afternoon two boxes of pug plants. They where:

- 40 – Rudbeckia "Toto"
- 40 – Dahlia "Harlequin"

I soaked the plug trays in water then filled 80 one litre pots with compost before planting a plug plant into each one. This done I put them into the ever crowded greenhouse to grow on. The only outstanding ordered plant is the Lonicera "Chic and Choc". Oh Happy Days!

The final countdown has begun!

Friday 2nd May and our holiday to Skiathos is only four week's away. This however, makes the next four weeks crucial to ensure that we leave the garden as best prepared for our two week absence as possible. Not only do we have to empty the greenhouse of all the pots of bedding plants and plant them in the beds/pots but reorganise the greenhouse so we can plant up our tomatoes, sweet pepper and cucumber plants waiting patiently in the sun lounge…

May 2014 in our Garden

Other tasks!

Once the new plants are planted out in the position where they will flower they will all need feeding with fertilizer to ensure that they put on the maximum growth before we leave to go on our holiday. We also need to think about conserving water in all the pots whilst we are away. The system we use is to put as many pots as possible into large trays and saucers to increase the chances of survival for as many plants as possible. We have also started to use grit on the top of each pot to help stop the pot drying out and conserve water. This is in case there is a dry warm spell in the UK while we are away. The system of using trays/saucers worked really well last year so here's hoping for the same outcome this year. Marble our cat has made a full recovery from his recent illness and along with our other cat Jasper will be spending their holiday at the local cattery called Cats Whiskers once again.

Our cats are blissfully unaware of their pending holiday

May 2014 in our Garden

All looks good to me!

Having spent some time planning and implementing what we needed to do before our holiday I set about the here and now by cutting the lawn and bank. After my exertions of cutting both the back lawn and front bank I had severe pain in my left knee (an old injury) so I went and had a rest on the decking with a nice cup of tea. The trouble is that my knee will now play me up all night so I will get very little sleep (oh poor me). The main thing that seems to cause my knee to react and give me severe pain is when I am pushing the mower at an angle whilst cutting the front grass bank. Susie has had the bright idea of getting me a strimmer which seems a very good idea indeed. I think we should get one as soon as possible.

The giver of life!

Every day I spend up to an hour watering the pots in the greenhouse and, if it has not rained, I need to water all of the plants in the beds and pots in the front and back garden. This is crucial to ensure that the life giving quality of water is provided to help the plants generate strong healthy new growth. It is great that we now have outside taps and hoses instead of having to use water pumps and cans to deliver the water to our plants…

May 2014 in our Garden

The birds!

Another of my daily tasks is to feed the birds. Oliver our pheasant is coming twice a day for his breakfast and afternoon tea. So while I take a rest after doing any garden tasks and recuperate on the decking with a nice drink I can watch all of the birds feeding. How good is that!

Plant update!

The new plug plants that I potted up yesterday and put in the greenhouse are all looking good and starting to put on new growth.

All of the 300 plus new plants in the greenhouse should be ready to plant out in our garden over the next two weeks I hope…

May 2014 in our Garden

The usual pattern!

Saturday 3rd May: Today is normally the day when we do our weekly shop. As luck would have it our local Tesco supermarket has a Dobbies garden centre attached. So after completing our shopping this morning we just had to (well me actually) have a walk around the garden centre.

No prizes given!

Yes you have guessed it I just had to have some more plants for the garden. This time we managed to get:

- Nemesia "Wisley Vanilla"
- Isotoma "Starshine Blue"

So even when we are doing our weekly food shopping I can still manage to get a few more plants for our garden. So there is no surprises there then!

I planted the new plants into two of the pots beneath the clematis next to our arbour when we got home…

May 2014 in our Garden

Getting ready for summer!

Sunday 4th May: It is now time to re-introduce the summer weekly plant feeding regime. I will need to use my watering can and put the powdered fertilizer dissolved into water into it to feed all pots and borders in the front and back gardens. I will also have to remember to do the same thing for the plants in the greenhouse. Next week we hope to plant all of the pots of seedlings, cuttings and plug plants into the garden pots and borders that are currently in the greenhouse.

Pots waiting on our patio for the new plants!

Once this is done it will be the turn of the fruit in the sun lounge to be moved into pots in the greenhouse. When we have done all of the above the fun will really begin. The fruit will require daily care as will the new plants in the beds and pots. Feeding the birds will also be a daily job. Plant feeding, dead heading and grass cutting will also need to be done regularly. All this will keep me very busy before we go on holiday…

May 2014 in our Garden

Watering the plants then it is time for a drink for us!

Monday 5th May: Today is a glorious day of sun and blue skies with just a few white fluffy clouds. After watering the greenhouse, borders and pots Susie and I settled down to sunning ourselves on the decking and having a few drinks!

Seats ready on the patio all we need now are the drinks!

Publish and be dammed!

Our friends Corri and Roy joined us for lunch. They are both writers and Roy is also a publisher of books as well! I asked Roy to review my recently completed draft of my first book **"Retiring to the Garden – Year ONE"** with a view to seeing if he would publish it for me? I would like to have it published as a paperback so I can give copies away to our friends and family. Both Roy and Corri loved the book and he immediately said **YES** he would publish it for me as a paperback and also as an E-book. I am proud of my first writing effort and with Roy's help I will now be able to call myself not only a gardener, watercolour artist, writer but also an author of a published book. How good is that. I am very sad to say Roy died in November 2018. He is greatly missed!...

May 2014 in our Garden

The man from the publishers (Roy) he says YES!

After Roy had said yes to publishing my first book he said that he will also, along with Corri, edit my draft for me and provide marketing and promotional support for my subsequent book and E-book launch. So once edited, printed and distributed via Amazon and other World Wide Web book distributors my book will become available anywhere in the World! I will also get thirty six copies of the finished printed paperback to do with as I please. This will mean that in a few short weeks I will be a published author. Not bad for an old retired person! This fills me with a great sense of pride that not only has our garden provided me with a sense of purpose, endless opportunities, fantastic blooms but has also been the catalyst and inspiration to write about my experiences in it… **What a result!**

Making my dream come true!

Much of the credit for my forthcoming book must go to Susie who has been a constant source of encouragement and has worked harder than me at ensuring that our garden exploits have been such a success.

Thank you Susie for making my dream come true

May 2014 in our Garden

Meanwhile back to our garden!

Tuesday 6th May: Today has been warm but wet. This is great because the rain water will not only save me having to water the plants (except in the greenhouse of course) but will give all of the garden plants a boast and help them grow healthier by having fresh rainwater instead of treated tap water for a change.

The multi-coloured greenhouse!

Susie had to go back to work today after the bank holiday break but before she did she helped me re-hang our multi-coloured plastic door curtain that we use in the inside of our greenhouse doorway in the summer:

The door curtain is made from multi-coloured strips of plastic ribbon so the greenhouse will not only benefit from the extra shade it will provide but when the door is open and the curtain is hanging down it will provide an effective screen to keep bugs and birds out the greenhouse and off my young plants. The door curtain has proved to be a cheap and effective way of achieving the above whilst adding interest and colour to the garden as a whole...

May 2014 in our Garden

The story so far!

Wednesday 7th May: Before we venture into the future it is time to reflect on the progress we have made so far in our garden this season.

Inside our sun lounge!

The only plants left in the sun lounge at the moment are the tomato, sweet pepper and cucumber plants and these are all ready for planting into their pots in the greenhouse next weekend.

Our front garden!

All of the pots in the front garden have been refreshed with new compost and most have been planted up and horticultural grit has been dressed on the top of each planted up pot. The front beds have both been dug over and all of the existing plants have been pruned back to encourage new growth. We will add more new plants from the greenhouse into each border and the remaining empty pots at the weekend. This will completed our planting plan for the front garden this season except the two wall baskets that are either side of our front door. These will remain empty until we come home from holiday when we will plant them up with petunias that we will need to get from a garden centre.

Our back garden decking and patio!

My watercolour painting of Rex…

The decking that we made last year has been treated and refurbished with some ornaments and three flower pots. these have been planted up and are now ready for all those lazy days of summer. The pots on the patio near the house have all been refreshed with new compost and either planted up and gritted or are still waiting for new plants from the greenhouse this coming weekend…

May 2014 in our Garden

Our back garden beds!

In all of the back garden beds the existing plants have all been pruned back to encourage new growth and they have also been fed with blood, fish and bone granules and also liquid fertiliser. Any gaps in the beds will be planted up with the new plants out of the greenhouse come the weekend.

Our greenhouse!

Currently the greenhouse is full to nearly overflowing point with new plants that we have nurtured for weeks. Most of these will be planted out in the beds and pots this coming weekend. A few will remain in the greenhouse and be planted into the flower trough that we made last year hoping that they will grow into suitable blooms that can be cut and displayed indoors. As previously mentioned, come the weekend, we will re-organise the greenhouse by placing the prepared fruit pots into deep plastic water trays (precaution to ensure they have enough water whilst we are away). This will then allow us to at last bring the tomato, sweet pepper and cucumber plants out of the sun lounge (Susie will be pleased) and plant them in the pots in the position where they will hopefully fruit happily all summer long!

May tulips…

Things of special note!

The new Fox Delphinium and Dahlia tubers that we planted earlier this year are all making up into strong healthy plants. The Fuchsias and Salvias that I propagated from cuttings over the winter are also doing very well. It's good when a plan comes together! This all signals the potential for a very colourful summer ahead…

May 2014 in our Garden

Rain stops play!

Thursday 8th May: It rained hard all day today so apart from watering the young plants in the greenhouse and feeding the birds I spent the rest of the day finalising the details for the publication of my first book.

First signs of new life!

Friday 9th May: The sky has cleared this morning and it is sunny so I ventured outside again to check for signs of new life in the dahlia pots on the patio. Dahlias are showing their first signs of growth in nine of the pots with only four still to raise their new shouts above the surface of the pots. I will leave them to get a bit bigger before I introduce horticultural grit around the top of the sprouting dahlias early next week. Having done my search for new life it was off to the supermarket to get our weekly shop a day earlier than usual so we can spend all of our time during the coming weekend to plant up our garden.

Mission accomplished!

After finishing the weekly shop and whilst still out in the car I just had to call in at a local garden centre just in case. This proved to be an inspired move on my behalf because they had two shrubs that we have been searching for, for a long time. These were:

- Myrtle (Luma) "Apiculata Glamlean Gold"
- Daph'ne "Odora Aureomarginate"

Alan happy with his new plants

May 2014 in our Garden

The shrubs!

The Myrtle has gold and green variegated leaves. It is an evergreen shrub with white flowers in July and the Daph'ne is a sweetly fragrant plant that has purplish pink and white flowers that flower in the late winter to early spring. The Daph'ne is also evergreen with dark glossy green and yellow edged foliage.

Whilst I was at the garden centre I also increased our plant/garden products world further with the following:

- Nemesia "Berries and Cream"
- 20 Oxalis Deppei "Iron Cross" bulbs
- 15 Gladiolus Callianthus "Murielae" bulbs
- 2 Coca Fibre liners 30 cm to fit into our outside flower bird cages
- 3 kg box of fish, blood and bone granular plant food

Mission accomplished I headed home to plant up my new found trophies! I will keep the newly acquired/planted myrtle and daph'ne plants in the carport until tomorrow morning

Our dog Poppy keeping an eye out in Shouldham Warren in May 2019

May 2014 in our Garden

The BIG WEEKEND!

Saturday 10th May: Today we had planned to empty the greenhouse of all our new young plants and sort out the trough and put the fruit pots in their allocated places in the greenhouse. After this we had planned to plant up all our new plants into pots and beds in the garden before transferring, at last, the tomato, sweet pepper and cucumber plants out of the sun lounge and into their pots in the greenhouse. This was why today should have seen the start of the big weekend of finally planting up all of our plants into where they will flower this season.

What happened to spoil it? - The British Weather of course!

Wet and windy: We got up at 6 am rearing to get started and of course it was wet and windy and the weather forecasted on the radio was that it would remain like this **ALL DAY!**

Great so it was second prize for me!

Because of the wind and rain I decided that I could at least plant up the Nemesia "Berries and Cream", Oxalis Deppei "Iron Cross" bulbs and the Gladiolus Callianthus "Murielae" bulbs that I got yesterday in the dry inside our carport.

A sun flower…

Just when I had finished planting the new plants (9 am) the sun came out. Would you believe it!…

May 2014 in our Garden

Great - It is FIRST prize for US after all!

So you lose some and then just when you think about giving up you only go and win the big one. The weather at 9.15 am changed from rain and wind to calm, dry and sunny so much for the weather forecasters!

The demarcation of effort (a democracy at work)!

It looked like it would remain fine and dry for some time so we decided to divide up the tasks that needed doing so that we could achieve our big weekend after all. I set about emptying the greenhouse of all of the young plants in pots and put the water trays and fruit pots in there place in the greenhouse. Then I planted these up with the fruit out of the sun lounge. Then I lined, composted, fertilised and put water retention gel into the trough in the greenhouse before planting this up with the seedlings that I had grown from seed and also some of the plug plants.

The trough in our greenhouse fully planted up and a rabbit in the long grass

May 2014 in our Garden

Susie swings into action!

Susie was planting all of the new plants that I had taken out of the greenhouse into the garden pots and beds.

This work took us five hours to complete but as we looked around our garden afterwards we could see that it had been time well spent although we may suffer some aches and pain later as a result!

We even had time to have a glass of wine or two in celebration of our achievements on the patio when we had finished before the weather took a turn for the worse and sent us scurrying once more inside to rest out of the now heavily falling rain at 4 pm...

May 2014 in our Garden

The BIG tidy up!

Sunday 11th May: We woke up this morning to guess what? **YES** you are right heavy rain! Was this going to stop us? **NO** because this is not a problem today as first and foremost the new plantings will really benefit from all this natural rain water. Secondly we only have tiding up jobs left to do today and these can be done either in the greenhouse or inside the carport.

Holidays are coming!

In the carport we were in the dry as we went about tidying up from yesterday's massive planting session. First we sorted out all of the empty plant pots from yesterdays massive planting session and stacked them in the racking in the greenhouse. Next we trimmed the overhanging liner that I had put into the trough in the greenhouse yesterday before planting it up with plants. Following this we re-potted the "Inca Gold" trailing sunflowers into larger pots and then stored them in a plastic deep water tray in the greenhouse because we will not be planting these outside into the beds until after we return home from holiday were I hope to be in the wet, warm sea!…

May 2014 in our Garden

Jobs (well) DONE!

That brings to a conclusion our big planting weekend when we planted our garden pots and beds and the greenhouse pots and trough up ready for the season ahead and we even had enough time to tidy up after ourselves despite all that the British weather could throw at us. All we need now is some hot sunny weather to mature our plants and stimulate them to bloom. Before we called it a day we fed all of the new plantings in the greenhouse and garden. All is now set for the season ahead…

The waiting game!

Monday 12th May: All of the patio potted dahlias are now through and making up nicely.

I have nipped out the shout above the first two pairs of leaves of the dahlias as this helps them to bush up and have more flowers. To finish the dahlia pots off I completed the topping of the last few pots with horticultural grit. Now that all of the borders and pots have been planted up and the fruit plants are in the greenhouse it does not mean that we are finished far from it now the next phase of the gardeners year commences. We will now have to keep the grass cut, feed the birds, weed the beds, water if required, feed the plants to promote growth and dead head flower blooms regularly. Such are the joys of being a gardener…

May 2014 in our Garden

Exciting times!

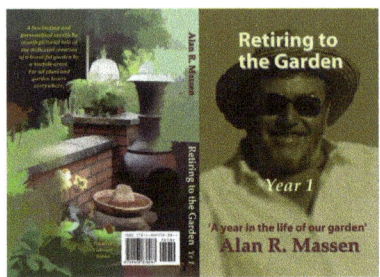

Tuesday 13th May: Today I gave Roy my publisher the final draft of my first book **"Retiring to the Garden – Year One"**. Roy and Corri will now edit this in preparation for it being sent off to the printers. Roy thinks that the finished published book could be available in about six to eight weeks time. So very soon I will become a published author. As you can understand this is a very exciting time for me and to think that soon others will be able to share with me the trials and tribulations of being a retired person with time on their hands. I hope that all the pleasure that I have gained from having the time to spend in our garden comes through in my book and those reading it may be inspired to spend more time in their own garden.

The final touches!

Now that I have given you my exciting news it is back to our garden where I finished planting up the front beds with the few plants that we had left over after planting up the back beds, pots and greenhouse. All that was left to do then was the final tidy up before retiring to the decking for a well earned rest and a nice cup of tea.

The crowd roared (well maybe)!

If there had been a spectator/crowd watching Susie and I working in our garden last weekend I am sure they would have given us a big roar of approval as we completed the planting up of all our beds, pots and greenhouse.

Reflections!

I have come to the conclusion that April and May are the hardest two months for the gardener in the whole of the gardening year…

May 2014 in our Garden

The Final fling!

Wednesday 14th May: After all our recent planting we still had a few pots that needed to be planted up. We left these so we could see what plants we had left over after our big planting out weekend. As I have already mentioned I used what few plants that we had left over to add extra colour into the front beds so we will need the following extra plants to make sure that every possible container is filled:

- 3 herb plants (Susie knows which ones she still needs)
- 1 packet of lettuce leaves seeds
- 4 plants for patio pots
- 3 plants for the bird cages
- 6 plants for the wall baskets

How sad this will mean that we will just have to make another trip to the garden centre (he-he-he) but we will leave this excursion until after we return from our holiday. This is because the containers that these plants are intended to fill are very susceptible to hot dry weather and so it would be prudent to wait until we return from holiday so we can ensure they get enough water…

While we are away the fox on the seat next to the shed will watch over our garden for us…

May 2014 in our Garden

Relaxing times!

Thursday 15th May: I am very much looking forward to being able to relax a lot more in the coming months as we have now completed the labour intensive jobs for this year's garden season. This does not mean however, that it will be all rest and no play as I will still have the back lawn and front bank grass to keep in check, the birds to keep fed and our developing plants will need watering and feeding regularly. Susie will continue to weed the beds and pots from time to time and hang out the washing at weekends but even so for both of us it will mean that we have more time to relax and enjoy the garden coming into bloom.

Susie hanging out the washing while Oliver asks for some more food!

Later in the season I will have to start dead heading again along with the other jobs mentioned above…

May 2014 in our Garden

Success of the Dahlias!

Friday 16th May: All of the dahlias that I planted earlier this year in the beds and pots have all come through now. More interesting still is that the dahlias that I removed from the garden and stored last winter before I re-potting them up this spring were the first to show. They are already making up into study young plants and are even flowering. I will defiantly be digging ALL of this years dahlias up and storing them inside so that I have more free plants next year.

There is more success too!

The success of the dahlias that I over wintered has been mirrored by the geraniums, begonias, fuchsias and salvias that I also over wintered but this time in their pots in the greenhouse. These plants also are making up into beautiful strong plants and yet again they hold the promise of lovely blooms at no cost. This really is the way forward…

May 2014 in our Garden

The way forward to save money!

As we have seen over wintering your prized plants rather than leaving them to be killed by the winter frosts is not only sensible but also cost effective. By harvesting our flowers seed, taking cuttings and digging up our tubers we have been able to propagate new life or extend the life of existing plants from one year to the next. All this has been made possible by having the greenhouse to over winter my seedlings and cuttings in as well as storage in our house (provided by the kind permission of Susie) to store our tubers, tender cuttings and to germinate seeds. Now that I know how successful this has been I can continue this practice in the years to come! Oh happy days!

Self sufficiency!

Never mind the good life (sorry an old TV comedy programme) I will become self sufficient for most of our garden plant requirements next season and for years to come.

Watercolour Painting of Monty…

Cracking the code!

I really feel that now I have cracked the code for being a successful gardener. We will only need to buy annual plants next year to give us that extra splash of colour in our pots and beds. Everything else in the garden pots and beds will be free plants nurtured from our own seeds, cuttings and tubers. Oh happy days! All of the above shows just how valuable Susie's gift of a greenhouse to me when I retired really was and we will have recouped its cost in no time by being able to grow most of our fruit and flower requirements in-house…

May 2014 in our Garden

The deep joy and rewards of dead heading!

Saturday 17th May: Anyone who has read my first book will know that I extolled the praises of dead heading extensively in there however, this is such an important gardening tip that I make no apology for covering it again here for any new readers. I started one of my favourite garden tasks today. It is called dead heading. This is were you go around your garden daily to remove all spent and/or tired blooms to encourage the plants to send out more flower buds, thereby, extending the flowering session. It has the added advantages of giving you the opportunity to observe the health of every plant so that you can either feed and/or water if required to ensure healthy plants every day. Usually at the start of the dead heading season I will get about half a bucket of dead heads increasing every day up until the middle of August to two full buckets per day. The buckets of dead heads I then put into my compost bin so nothing goes to waste and the compost this produces will go back onto the beds next spring. I will stop dead heading my plants in late August to allow them to make seed so that Susie can go around and collect them for me (she always collect's, bags and labels the seed for me). We store these in a dry dark indoor cupboard over winter. This is what nature intended and allows the plants to achieve their destiny by the reproduction of the next generation. Then in February and March I will use the seeds to propagate more free plants for the coming new season. I did this last year and many of the plants in our garden this year are as a direct result of this process.

Painting of Mousehole in Cornwall

May 2014 in our Garden

Go on give it a go!

I strongly recommend that you start dead heading, leaving the plants to produce seed in late summer, collecting the seed then re-sowing these next spring. By taking the above action plus taking cuttings, dividing up large perennials and removing and storing your tubers you too will have free plants next year too!

Getting ready for the off!

After dead heading today Susie and I placed saucers, buckets and trays under as many of our garden pots as we could. This is to help our plants survive while we are away on holiday. We did the same thing last year and it was really successful. We finished gardening for the day by moving as many pots into the shaded part of our patio as this will also help them to conserve water while we are away. Then it was time to relax on the decking with a few drinks in hand. I can not guarantee that this will work for you but it has for us and I would recommend that you try it if you have to leave your garden for any length of time…

Mamma Mia!

Sunday 18th May: The rose "Mamma Mia" that we planted into Susie flower bed is now a strong healthy bush and we are looking forward to seeing it flower come July. We bought it because its name reminded us of our paradise island of Skiathos (see above) where the film by the same name was part filmed…

May 2014 in our Garden

Meeting old friends!

Now that we are less than two weeks before we arrive in Skiathos we are getting very excited and looking forward to seeing once again all our Skiathan friends Yellis, Katherine. George, Katia, Yannis, Alexei, Yannis. Ervin, Dori, Tim, Michel, Vangelis. We are also looking forward to seeing George and Eve of the Mythos Café Bar again. To top this all off our friends Karl, Anna, Alistair, Issy, Andrew and Lynn will also be there once again. **So the gang will be all present and correct…**

As we sit on our decking admiring our Mamma Mia rose and dream of our holiday it is hard to believe that in twelve short days we will be jetting off from Gatwick airport back to our paradise island of Skiathos once more.

Back to reality!

Before any of this can happen we still have much to do to ensure that the garden is best prepared for our absence. We must weed, feed, water, mow and generally nurture our new plants. That said it is very sunny and warm today so that can all wait for another day. More wine I think!…

May 2014 in our Garden

Disaster strikes!

Monday 19th May: Early this morning whilst stepping out of the greenhouse disaster struck. I must have twisted when stepping over the lip out of the greenhouse because I suddenly felt a searing pain in my right knee. It was so painful that I could hardly walk so I had to Scream (yes the pain was that bad) for Susie to come and help me. Springing into action Susie immediately got a lounger chair out of our shed put it on the decking and helped me hobble over and sat me down. As it was over 23°C today I was able to sit out on the decking and try and recover. Susie made me a cup of tea and there I sat waiting for the pain to subside. The pain remained acute and I later found out from the Doctor that I had damaged my medial ligament and with our holiday only a few days away I hoped that it would soon settle down so we are still able to go! Luckily I have several knee supports and a walking stick to hand which I sometimes use because of the problems that I have with my damaged left knee so hopefully one of these will help me get about until the right knee gets better and heals up.

My watercolour painting of Susie…

Some good news at least!

To cheer me up whilst I was incapacitated on the decking Susie decided to go out and get us the few plants that we still wanted to complete our pots and cages instead of waiting to get them until after we hopefully return from holiday! She returned with some lovely plants that she planted up before bring me a nice ice cold beer and we watched the swallows perform acrobatics in the sky for the rest of the day…

May 2014 in our Garden

A.W.O.L. (absent without leave)!

Tuesday 20th May: Oliver our pheasant has gone absent without leave for the last five days. At 7 pm yesterday he finally reappeared so after getting a good telling off by me we welcomed him back and gave him a good feed.

Sticking it out!

Alan with his stick…

Sleepy head…

I am now using a walking stick to help me hobble about (the knee is still very painful). Susie has ordered a pair of special knee patella supports for me to help hold the knee in place to aid its recovery. In the meantime Susie will have to do all of the daily garden, household and other related tasks that I usually do as well as her full time job. Poor girl but she always has a big smile for me! We hope that with the knee support and by using a walking stick and with as much rest as possible over the next 10 days I will still be able to go on holiday. Please keep your fingers crossed for me and Susie at this difficult time…

May 2014 in our Garden

Another first for our garden!

Wednesday 21st May: Our lime and lemon trees planted last year are both bearing their first ever fruit. This is another first for our garden and one that we will be able to celebrate with the ripe fruit very soon. Even with a painful knee I could still see the positives and opportunities that our own ripe lime and lemons bring to our summer drinking favourites of gin and tonic for Susie and Cuba Libra (more on this cocktail later) for me. It was again warm and sunny today and the temperature was over 20°C. I sat at the patio resting my knee and finished my Sue Grafton book "W is for Wasted". It is very good if like me you enjoy reading private detective stories.

Going back!

On a flight of fancy having completed the above book I then decided to re-read Lee Child's latest book "Never go back". I can always read his books time and time again as they are so good…

May 2014 in our Garden

Wishing and Hoping!

I hope that when my first book is published someone will enjoy my offering just as much as I enjoy reading other authors work. I do hope so.

Hard at work!

Not me you understand (poorly knee) but the pair of blackbirds that are using our garden as a feeding station to feed their newly hatched baby. They can be seen (from my seat on the patio or decking) repeatedly collecting worms and other food stuff to take back to their young . It is amazing just how much they can cram into their beaks at any one time. The blackbirds really work very hard and are fine parents.

A watching brief!

Sitting on the patio also gives me the time to just sit and look at all the flowers and watch swallows make circles in the sky. Everything in the garden is about two weeks ahead of where it was last year because of the mild winter and this means I can therefore admire all of the flowers that I usually miss while we are away on holiday…

May 2014 in our Garden

The fruits of our labours!

In the greenhouse the newly planted tomato, sweet pepper and cucumber (grown from seed) are beginning to make up into good strong plants. The new trough that I planted up last weekend is already full of healthy plants and some of them are even flowering already.

The border country!

In our borders (beds) the roses are coming into flower and the Californian Orange Poppy is flowering and as a result they need dead heading daily (Susie is doing this for me because of my poorly knee). The Red Giant Poppy is also flowering and is magnificent.

Many of the flowers in our garden are in bloom

May 2014 in our Garden

Little things mean a lot!

Thursday 22nd May: It is often the little things you do that mean a lot. This year I have topped every pot in our garden with horticultural grit which has proved most successful and took very little time to do. It not only looks good but it also suppresses the weeds and helps the plant conserve water. Try it and see…

Other little things!

The other little things that I am trying this year are:

- Marigolds companion planted with the tomatoes
- Using blood, fish and bone fertiliser in every hole before we plant our young plants to give each plant a boast
- Growing cut flowers in the trough in the greenhouse for the house

I will let you know how these new trials work out later in the year. Meanwhile back to the Jack Reacher book.

My painting of a
Tiger on the hunt…

Additional support arrives!

My patella knee supports arrived by post today. I immediately fitted one of these to my right knee and hey presto my knee felt much more stable but it was still very painful when walking. The holiday is looking like a goer thankfully now so with my walking stick, new support and pain killing drugs (from the Doctor) I now feel confident that I will be able to limp along until I get home.

Getting strapped up!

Friday 23rd May: I have been wearing my knee support for 24 hours now (not whilst in bed) and the knee continues to feel more stable so things are looking good holiday wise…

May 2014 in our Garden

It is all down to Susie once more!

Due to my current mobility problems Susie has volunteered to do the final preparation jobs in our garden ready for our departure. These are: Mow the back garden lawn - Fill up the water trays in the greenhouse - Feed and water all of the plants. Once these are done I am fairly confident that we (I mean Susie) have done all that we can to keep our garden healthy while we are away. Fingers crossed!

Fantastic!

Saturday 24th May: This morning while I was sitting on the patio with a cup of coffee I glanced up into our silver birch and there feeding on the nuts was a Greater Spotted Woodpecker. How fantastic was that. I sat very quietly and still and he stayed feeding for about 10 minutes before flying off. This really is one of nature's greatest sights. Lucky me!

Making ready!

Sunday 25th May: I am still not mobile enough so Susie cut the back lawn today then she filled up the water trays in the greenhouse before feeding and watering everything.

Cats eyes:

She really is a diamond that girl!

After all the above jobs were done Susie and I decided that it was time for both of us to relax and soak up the rays as it was clear skies and 26°C. We had a few cold drinks, as you do, some nibbles and watched the swallows darting around the sky as we sat on the decking…

May 2014 in our Garden

Armed and dangerous!

Monday 26th May: Today Susie was armed and dangerous as she took our battery driven hedge cutter and removed the bottom two feet off our Kilmarnock Willow that is in the top back garden bed.

Ginny came too…

Later the same day our daughter Ginny joined us for lunch on the patio and stayed the rest of the afternoon.

The plant hunters!

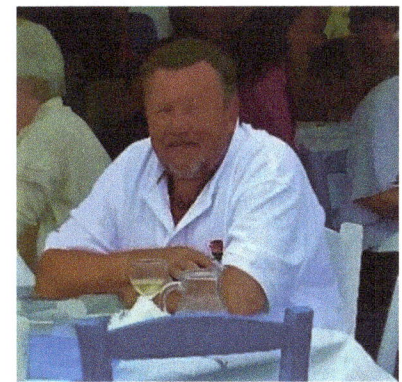

Tuesday 27th May: Today we woke up to cold and rain so as I was now able to hobble about a little bit better Susie suggested that she took me out as I had not been outside our garden for more than ten days. When she said "we could go hunt for some new plants" I grabbed my walking stick and put on my knee support and we headed out. I had to take it carefully getting in and out of her car and also I only walked around one garden centre (very restrained of me yes – but my knee did really hurt – **"you poor old thing"** Susie would say)…

May 2014 in our Garden

What did we buy!

Well it will be no surprise to you my reader that yes we did manage to find some new additions for our garden. These were: Goultheria "Procumbens" - Herb "Coriander" - Herb "Red Basil" - Dahlia "Orange beauty" - Serena "Angelonia Purple" - Scaevola "Zig Zag" - Fuchsia "Fairy Lavender". We returned home and wondered just where we were going to plant them but fortunately I still had some empty pots beside the house so Susie planted them in those. Problem solved. Susie then planted the outside trough near the arbour with lettuce leave seeds so that they will be ready when we return from holiday.

Susie…

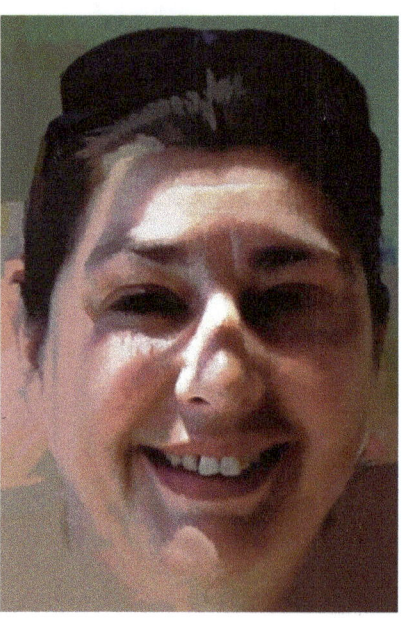

Then there was the truss!

Not a truss for me you understand but a truss in our greenhouse. Well actually quite a few trusses on our tomato plants. Susie spotted them when she watered the greenhouse for me. There were even two cucumbers on the cucumber plants!

And there was more!

The sweet peppers grown from seed have begun to produce flowers. That will become fruit in the near future. This is great news and soon we will be able to dine on our own produce once more. Oh happy days…

May 2014 in our Garden

Room(s) with a view!

Wednesday 28th May: Every four weeks or so our window cleaner Kevin comes around and cleans all of our house windows for us. He often spares a few minutes with me to have a cup of tea and a chat and I enjoy our conversations very much and always look forward to his visits. The work he performs for us is absolutely essential because clean windows means better views for us of our garden and the wild life when it is to wet to go outside. Well done that man…

Get ready!

Thursday 29th May: As the pain in my knee begins to ease I have been able to do a little watering and feeding. I was even able to replenish the bird feeders today. Then of course it was time for a rest and a read.

Get Steady!

After a suitable rest and recuperation break I was able to finish the last day in our garden before flying off by taking down the hanging baskets and putting them into buckets of water and then taking a last look at some of the flowers in our garden.

Now all is ready so let's GO…

May 2014 in our Garden

It's Holiday time!

Friday 30th May: Today was the day that we set off for our paradise island of Skiathos. I get so excited on the morning when we leave for our holiday. We got up at 4 am and armed with my walking stick and knee support on we set off for Gatwick airport at 5 am arriving at just after 7.30 am. Our flight to Skiathos with Thomson was not scheduled to take off until 12.20 pm so we had nearly 5 hours to wait at the airport. This may seem a long time to wait and people might think that we get there far too early but this is intentional on our part. For those of you that are in the know will understand that by leaving so early we give ourselves a fair chance that the M 25 will be reasonably clear (this road is notorious for having long delays during peak times). We have done the same thing for the last few years and to date our cunning plan has worked beautifully. So with time on our hands at the airport we get rid of our cases as soon as possible and then go and have a full English breakfast and then we have time for several cigarette breaks before going through to the departure lounge.

Coming in to land at Skiathos and a Greek cat

May 2014 in our Garden

Arriving in paradise!

Our Thomson plane took off on time at 12.20 pm and landed at Skiathos International Airport at 15.50 pm or 17.50 pm local time. We always use the coach provided by the tour operator (Thomson) for our onward transfer to our hotel and we arrived at Troulos Bay Hotel at about 6.30 pm local time. As we had been travelling for more than 7 hours we rested after retrieving our cases off the coach (Susie did this as I was in quite a lot of pain by this point) and we rested on the wall outside our hotel reception (this was more a need for me to have a cigarette really).

Meeting and Greeting!

TROULOS BAY HOTEL TEAM - SKIATHOS

Our delay in not entering the hotel straight away had not gone unnoticed first George the hotel manager came out. The smile that he gave us when he spotted us was worth all the long hours of travelling. He came down the ramp to greet us with hugs and kisses to both our cheeks and then took our cases into reception to get Dori to take them up to our room. The next out was Head of Security and Reception Yannis who again greeted us warmly with hugs and kisses before escorting us into reception to complete the formalities and to give us our room key. We were in room 318 as usual and after making the arduous journey up the stairs to the top floor (it is only one floor up – so stop moaning) we opened our room to find our cases already there waiting for us. It is at this point that Susie smiled at me and said "look at what they have done for us this year"…

May 2014 in our Garden

The present(s)!

On the table top under the mirror there was a large bowl of cut fresh roses (talk about making you feel at home) and a bottle of Cretan white wine (our favourite),

That is not ALL!

On the wall next to our bed was hung one of my watercolour paintings that I gave the hotel back in 2010. Tell me how many people go away on holiday and go into their hotel room to find one of their works of art proudly displayed on their wall (not many me thinks). There are other examples of my watercolour art displayed in Georges office and several in the bar, lounge and reception area.

Back to our holiday!

After all this excitement you would think that it could not get any better than that but you would be wrong because what followed next is one of my favourite moments of the entire holiday. We walk hand in hand out onto our balcony to wonder at the fantastic view of the beach, Island, sea with the large island of Evia in the distance. This is truly a magical moment. This done Susie went off to the shop just up the road (I usually go but my knee and all) whilst I unpacked as best as I could. We always take our own coffee and tea bags as well as a kettle so we can make our own drink as and when we want. Susie came back with milk and bottled water (as the local water is not to the British taste buds) so we could have a cupper before turning in…

May 2014 in our Garden

The hotel restaurant!

After a quick shower it was downstairs for an evening meal. We always sit on the front row of tables looking out to sea (just like Shirley Valentine) in the restaurant. The view is to die for and it includes free of charge a dramatic flying display but more about that later.

This year the restaurant staff include, as usual, our very good friend Ervin who has been at the hotel for many years. He is ably assisted by Tim, Michel and Vangelis. We will have to wait until tomorrow to see the other family members that run the hotel. We had a nice meal, some wine and enjoyed the view but following a very long day of travelling we went up to our room early to catch up on some sleep. It was great to be finally here and we made the time to sit on our balcony for a little while before going to bed. I had a cup of tea and Susie had a coffee listening to the unique Greek sounds and smells that make Greece such a lovely place to be on a hot summer's night…

May 2014 in our Garden

The first full day of our holiday!

Saturday 31st May: We were up at 7 am (old habits die hard) and had a walk along the beach before enjoying a coffee/tea on our balcony before starting our first full day on our paradise island in our normal manner! The first job of the day is to take down the framed painting that I painted during the winter (three paintings in one frame) that we present as a gift to everyone at the hotel Yellis, Katherine, George, Katia, Yannis, Alexei (receptionist), Ervin (head waiter) Tim, Michel, Vangelis (waiters), Dori (pool, beach and gardener) and Yannis (head of security), they all work so hard to run the hotel like clockwork.

This year's offerings!

I give them one of my watercolour paintings as a gift on the first day and by the afternoon it is up in the lounge of the hotel. No greater complement could I get...

May 2014 in our Garden

Oh Vienna!

This morning our very good friends Karl and Anna from Vienna in Austria have arrived:

As is our custom we exchange gifts. Karl and Anna gave us some Vienna biscuits and some chocolates we gave them a DVD of Skiathos and two of my paintings. Talking to Karl he told me that when he was 17 he represented Austria in two international football matches. He also proudly told me that he signed two autographs (one of which was for Anna). He is truly a remarkable man. Karl and Anna have now been married for more than fifty years so that was a very good autograph he gave all those years ago! We congratulate them both. After seeing them it was time to walk up the road (me with knee support and walking stick in hand) to catch the local bus. We do this on the first day of our holiday every year. The bus stop is by the shop where Susie got yesterdays supplies...

May 2014 in our Garden

Out and About!

The local bus that runs along the coast road (the only road along the Island) into Skiathos Town only takes about 25 minutes to make the journey from one end of the island to the other.

Skiathos Island promotional!

Skiathos is the best known of the Sporades Islands. People are drawn by the allure of its beaches along with pretty villages, pine covered hills and a perfect climate. We always stay at The Troulos Bay Hotel because Troulos is the best beach and our hotel is right on the beach.

Skiathos Town!

Skiathos Town is beautiful with its churches, statue and lovely harbours (the new port and the old port)…

May 2014 in our Garden

While we are in Skiathos Town!

We always go into town at least four or five times during our stay on Skiathos. Once there we head for our favourite café in the Old Port called the Mythos Cafe.

THE CAFÉ MYTHOS COCKTAIL-BAR - THE OLD PORT - SKIATHOS TOWN

There we sit and watch the world go by while having maybe some food but always a few drinks (sometimes more than just a few).

The Mythos Café!

Over the years we have made friends with the family that owns and runs the Mythos Café and as at the hotel we always take them a small gift (this is a local Greek custom). This year we gave them a DVD of Skiathos, some personalised key rings, fridge magnet and some of my art work. They were so please with their gifts they would not let us pay for any drinks or food (and we had quite a lot of both). Nikos the waiter even gave us a special dessert that he had made himself. So after several hours as their guests and after shopping up the high street (for Susie you understand) it was back on the bus and back to the hotel for an evening meal at our table before tea/coffee on the balcony before bedtime. **A lovely end to a great first full day on Paradise!…**

June 2014 in our Garden

Our Island of Paradise - Skiathos!

First day on the beach!

Sunday 1st June: When we got up this morning the weather was overcast but it soon cleared to reveal blue sky spotted with fluffy white clouds. As it looked like it was going to be a nice day we decided to spend it on Troulos Bay beach. We filled our thermal lined beach bag with a litre bottle of cold water (yes we have a refrigerator in our room) and went down to see Alexei on reception for some beach towels and a sun bed ticket (eight Euro's) before arriving on the beach at 9.50 am. The sun was very hot and the sea was quite cold but we enjoyed them both. We had lunch in the hotel beach side restaurant. It was good to chat to Ervin, Tim and Michel the waiters to see how their year had been. We came off the beach at about 6 pm and decided to have our evening meal on the balcony (we went and got some filled rolls and crisp from the shop up the road) and have the wine the hotel kindly left us in our room on the first day. This meant that we could also watch the falcons flying around the bay/sea at 8.45 pm from our vantage point. They perform one of nature's great shows soaring in the sky and just enjoying themselves every evening. There are about twelve to fourteen of them at any one time in the sky over our balcony. They just glide around enjoying the last of the day's thermals before flying back into the wooded hills that surround Troulos Bay. After a lazy full day on the beach and after eating our meal and wine on the balcony it was time to have a nice shower and then a cup of tea on the balcony before turning in for the night…

June 2014 in our Garden

Watching!

Monday 2nd June: We watched Dori cleaning the pool this morning from our balcony. He works very hard but always has the time to smile and wave as he works either in the garden, pool or on the beach. It is very restful to sit and watch others work in such a beautiful backdrop setting as Troulos. Today we had another lazy day on the beach and had our evening meal in the hotel restaurant again in our front row seats so we could watch the falcons flying display before once again retiring up to our balcony for tea/coffee before turning in after another hard day (well someone's got to do it!).

Rango Tango is coming!

Andy…

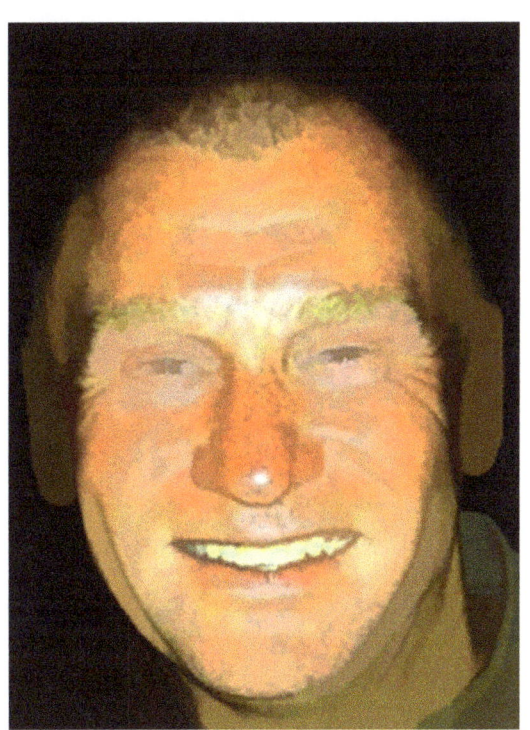

Tuesday 3rd June: Today more of our friends will arrive. We are very much looking forward to seeing once again Alistair and Issy from Scotland and Andrew (Rango Tango as Dori calls him because of the way he plays tennis) and Lynn from Sheffield. Today the rain fell out of the sky in torrents so we spent the day on our balcony reading and watching the swallows (just like at home) dip into the pool (not just like at home) and then at 2 pm **IT HAPPENED**…

June 2014 in our Garden

Dolphins ahoy!

As we were sitting on our balcony watching the rain fall onto the sea Susie suddenly said: "Look there in front of the island I can see three dolphins swimming towards Skiathos Town do you see them"? YES… This was the first time in all the years we have been going to Troulos Bay Hotel that we had seen any dolphins swimming in the sea just off the beach. We were truly delighted.

The grand entrance!

It was 4 pm and we were still sitting on the balcony and the rain was still falling, seeing the dolphins had really cheered us up considerably and now the welcome sound of the next door balcony door being slide open heralding the arrival of Andrew and Lynn. Yes they were next door to us as usual and a short time later Alistair and Issy appeared on the balcony beyond. Alistair and Issy gave us a bottle of wine and we gave them a DVD of Skiathos, fridge magnet and three of my paintings as a welcome gift. Andrew and Lynn gave us a bottle of champagne, ashtray, tea towel and some herbs as a gift and we gave them (yes you have guessed it!) a DVD of Skiathos, fridge magnet and three of my paintings.

We all said our hellos and then the rain stopped. Andrew invited us down to the pool bar for a welcome drink. Later we all went off to change for dinner. Andrew and Lynn joined us for a meal in the restaurant before Susie and I retired to our balcony…

June 2014 in our Garden

We are off to Town!

Wednesday 4th June: In the morning we decided to spend the day in Skiathos Town as the weather was still overcast. So armed with my trusty knee support and walking stick we went and caught the bus into town.

The first port of call was as usual the Mythos Café Bar in the Old Port for a few drinks and some lunch before Susie left me there to have just a few more Mythos (Greek beer) while she went up the shopping street to see what delights she could find. She returned with one or two small touristy things and after having one last drink with George and family at the café I hobbled (my knee was quite painful after all my walking and drinking) back to catch the local bus to return to the hotel for our evening meal, falcons, and tea on the balcony before bedtime.

The birthday girl!

Thursday 5th June. Today was Susie's birthday and to mark this occasion I had smuggled a small gift and a card in our luggage for her. I had bought her a silver and enamelled broach. As we sat on our balcony the next door balcony door opened and there was Andrew and Lynn clutching presents, card, bottle of sparkly (with glasses) and big grins to also wish Susie a happy birthday. Andrew opened the champagne and we all toasted Susie… A happy birthday… They gave Susie a heart shaped necklace that was lovely. They also gave us two beautiful cakes to have with our afternoon tea so not a bad start to her day. To spend your birthday in a beautiful location with good friends and being able to drink several glasses (they were small glasses) of bubbly first thing in the morning on your balcony makes for a very happy birthday indeed…

June 2014 in our Garden

A big night out!

We spent the day on the beach feeling a bit heady but none the less happy until 4.30 pm when we came off the beach had a shower and got dressed up for Susie's big night out. Tonight we are going to Skiathos Town with Andrew and Lynn to celebrate Susie's birthday. We had decided to go to Ervin's (our head waiter at the hotel) brother's restaurant the Bakaliko (his name is Bello) right on the shores of Skiathos Towns New Port where he is the head chef.

We also went there last year and enjoyed it very much. The Bakaliko restaurant is used by the locals to eat in the evenings and is reputed to be the best food on the Island. We can only but agree. Well done Bello. The four of us got a taxi down to the ferry port entrance (to save my poor knees) and walked around to the Mythos Café Bar for a pre-dinner drink before heading for Bello's restaurant for Susie's birthday dinner. Bello cooked us a great meal and gave us free wine and sweet. After thanking him we strolled back to the bus stop and went back to Troulos Bay Hotel to have a nightcap (well a few actually) in the hotel lounge with George. We told Ervin when we got back just how good our meal had been and how well Bello had treated us and he was very pleased. A very good day was had by all and Susie said she had enjoyed our night out very much and she said she was well pleased with all her lovely presents…

June 2014 in our Garden

The earth moved for us all (well almost all of us)!

Friday 6th June: After our busy day yesterday we spent today relaxing on the beach and in the sea which was beginning to warm up at last. At 3 pm whilst lying on our sun beds the earth moved (tremors actually) for everyone on the beach. There were two violent vibrations through the surface of the beach. It lasted for just a few moments. We later found out that there had been an earthquake on the sea bed off Skiopolos which is about 4 km from Skiathos. It measured 4.4 on the Ricter scale. So in the last few days we have seen dolphin off shore at Troulos for the first time and had earth tremors too… We all soon settled back to our sunbathing and swimming none the worse for our experience. Lynn had missed all this excitement because she was out swimming in the sea at the time and said that she had felt nothing (I don't know if she believed us when we told her of the tremors)!

The famous beach tennis tournament begins!

At 4 pm Dori marched up the beach carrying two bats and a ball ready for Rango Tango (Andrew) and him to commence what will be a daily event. The much heralded beach tennis tournament. This involves Dori hitting the ball as hard as he can (not without a certain level of skill) to (at) Rango Tango. Andrew more often than not returns these thunderbolts much to Dori's amazement. It is great for us less active types to lay there and see the effort these two titans put into their match. It is however, not for the faint hearted as you have to keep on you toes (well sit up on your sun bed actually and watch attentively) because sometimes the ball would fly off the bat straight at you! After all this excitement it was an early dinner in the hotel restaurant, a sit on our balcony to watch the flying display and then an early night…

June 2014 in our Garden

Knee up-date!

Saturday 7th June: Today my right knee seems to have settled down at last and I can manage to walk down to the pool bar, beach and restaurant (that's good then isn't it!) without my walking stick but still with my knee support on. I think this improvement is largely down to the sun and swimming in the beautiful clear blue sea. It could be another story when we return to the damp, cold and wet that is so often the case in England. Meanwhile we spent another day on the beach poor things. Susie goes down each morning at about 8 am (towel duty which I normally would do but yes you know by now my poorly knee) to put our beach towels onto one of the beds on the front row of the sun beds nearest the sea so I do not have to walk (hobble) to far to get in the sea. We watched the daily tennis match at 4 pm before going for a swim in the hotel pool and having a drink (or two) at the pool bar before going to our room to relax on the balcony, watch the world go by, then have a shower before going down for our evening meal. We had a drink at the hotel bar with George the hotel manager before going in to eat and guess what they do Cuba Libra cocktails here too (just like being back home)! He used a whole lime and a very large measure of Bacardi (white rum) with just a splash of cola. It was strong but it reminded me of sitting in our garden back home

We had our evening meal in the hotel restaurant with Ervin, Tim, Michel and Vangelis working tonight everything ran smoothly. Fresh sea bass was tonight's treat and it was lovely. We watched the falcons as usual before retiring (like in the title of my book) to our balcony (not garden as in my book) for a cup of tea/coffee and looking up at the evening stars before it was bedtime…

June 2014 in our Garden

Walking on the beach!

Sunday 8th June: We woke up at 7 am to thunder, sunshine and rain this morning and a beautiful rainbow so when it stopped raining we went straight down and had a walk on the sea shore. We just got back to our balcony and the heavens opened and it rained once more. By 9.30 am it was sun, sun, sun and so we grabbed our beach towels, sun bed ticket and it was back to sunbathing and swimming for us. We watched the daily tennis match at 4 pm before going for a swim in the hotel pool and having a drink at the pool bar before going to our room to relax on the balcony, watch the world go by, then had a shower before going to catch the bus to go into town for our evening meal. Susie and I had a walk along the Old Port then we decided to go to Ervin's brother's restaurant the Bakaliko for our evening meal as we enjoyed it so much the other day. Bello again cooked a great meal and gave us a free sweet and wine once more so we had a great time. Then it was the bus home and just time for a quick drink in the hotel bar with George before retiring to our balcony for tea/coffee before bed time…

Thunder and lightning!

Monday 9th June: There was a tremendous thunder and lightning storm over night that had kept us awake so we got up very tired but the sun was now up and the signs of the heavy rain had disappeared so it was down to the beach once more. We watched the daily tennis match at 4 pm before going for a swim in the hotel pool and having a drink (or two) at the pool bar before going to our room to relax on the balcony, watch the world go by, then had a shower before going somewhere for our evening meal…

June 2014 in our Garden

Making up our minds!

We decided to eat at the hotel restaurant tonight as we were both tired after another glorious day of swimming and sunbathing (yes it stayed sunny all day). The staff told us that another storm was predicted for tonight so after our dinner we went up early to our balcony to watch the falcons, have a nice cup of tea and then it was early to bed…

The NO SHOW!

Tuesday 10th June: Well the predicted storm never came last night so waking refreshed at 7 am and after sitting on our balcony for an hour or so it was off to the beach (some 10 metres outside the hotel door) at 9 am. After setting up our front row sun beds we went for a walk along the beach…

There be treasure!

During our daily walks along the beach we like to look for treasure. Today we found a large heart shaped stone, some smaller shinny stones, and some pine cones during our walk which we put into our bag when we got back to our sun beds. We will comb the beach most days of our holiday and therefore, go home with quite a little hoard of such treasures. These items we will take home with us and make a display of Skiathos treasures to complement the large beach pebbles that we found and brought home from Mousehole, Cornwall in 2012. They will act as a visual reminder of all the happy times we have spent on the paradise coast of Skiathos…

June 2014 in our Garden

Old Boys Ramblings from the sun bed!

We are in the last few days of our holiday and every day seems to go by quicker than the last. So lying on the sun bed it is often at this stage of the holiday that I think it would be great to be able to live permanently on Skiathos and spend all my time doing just this… But just when you are beginning to slip into a blissful dream someone or something comes along and spoils it!!!

Look Out it's that time again!

4 pm and time for the daily tennis match which is always a lively and often noisy affair. Still maybe it is time to stop dreaming and spend my time watching out for flying missiles called tennis balls.

Time for a Swim!

After all this excitement we went for a swim in the hotel pool and had a drink (or two) with Andrew, Lynn and Dori at the pool bar before going to our room to relax on the balcony. From our vantage point we could see the hotel cats (a usual feature in all Greek restaurants) playing before the arduous work begins of finding their supper. The British will feed me they must think and I can often be seen doing just that. Giving them tip bits off my plate for their supper. After a shower we went down and had a drink at the hotel bar with George the hotel manager before going in to eat in the hotel restaurant along with the cats… Following our normal pattern we watched the flying display by the falcons whilst having our meal. When we came to pay for our meal we discovered that Alistair and Issy had already paid for the wine that we had had with our dinner. We thanked them for their kindness before retiring to our balcony for yes you have guessed it tea, star gazing and then it was time for bed…

June 2014 in our Garden

Waking up in paradise!

Wednesday 11th June: We were up at 6.45 to see from our balcony that another glorious blue sky was awaiting us. You just can not beat waking up to paradise however, soon will come the day when we will have to leave all this and return to our own garden paradise. Not to bad then! After sitting on the balcony for a couple of hours it was off to the centre of Troulos village for us today. To get there (knee support and walking stick in hand- just in case) we set off up the road from the hotel, past the shop and bus stop and turn right at the T junction.

Up up and away!

Then it's up the road, passed the Victoria Bar where we will have a coffee and a rest on the way back and up to the main village centre. At this junction there are several general purpose shops and a couple of gift shops and a restaurant. This constitutes the laid back centre of Troulos.

There are babies crying at the Troulos road junction too!

Under the eves of many of the shops at this junction can be seen swallows nests. Each one contains several hungry baby swallows waiting for their mum and dad to come swooping in with more tasty morsels. As you stand there the swallows continually dive in and feed their young and almost immediately they leave once more to find more food. On this walk you also get to see many of the local wild flowers, bugs and butterflies which make's this a walk well worth while. Having partaken of the shopping opportunity offered in the local shops we returned to the hotel after taking our usual coffee break at the Victoria Bar on the way back down the hill…

June 2014 in our Garden

Back in the old routine!

Once back at the hotel (11 am) we adjourned back to the sun bed on the beach for more sunbathing and swimming. 4 pm and it was time once more for the daily tennis match. After all this excitement we went for a swim in the hotel pool and had a drink (or two) with Andrew and Lynn at the pool bar before going to our room to relax on the balcony.

After a shower we went down and had a drink at the hotel bar with George the hotel manager before going in to eat in the hotel restaurant along once more with the cats… Following our normal pattern we watched the wonderful flying display by the falcons while having our meal. We later, as is our way, retired to our balcony for yes you have guessed it more tea/coffee and a bit of star gazing before bedtime bed!

Almost time to go!

Thursday 12th June: We were woken up this morning by heavy rain and thunder. The sea was completely flat and calm and everywhere was very quite between the thunder claps. We sat on our the balcony with a cup of tea/coffee watching the sea in the hope that we would see some more dolphins again! No such luck but it was great fun watching all the Brit's rushing out to collect their already deposited towels and when the rain stopped at 9 am rushing back out again too put them out again. We hoped for their sake that it did not start raining again (tongue in cheek)…

June 2014 in our Garden

Keeping the cats amused!

The Troulos Bay Hotel cats sat bemused to see all of these scantily dressed people rushing about putting towels down, then up and then down again. The sun came back out at 9.30 so Susie and I went beach combing before taking our places on the beach sun beds once more.

At the appointed hour!

4 pm was the appointed hour and once again the daily tennis match commenced. We will miss this daily event as we are going home tomorrow (I know it is all very sad). After watching our last match we went for a swim in the hotel pool and had frappes with Andrew, Lynn at the pool bar before going to our room to relax on the balcony. We are meeting Andrew and Lynn for our last night's meal tonight so after a shower we went down to the pool bar to share with Andrew and Lynn the bottle of champagne and some nibbles that they had bought Susie for her birthday before having dinner with them in the hotel restaurant.

The last supper!

Yannis had been to the fish market early that morning and got Andrew and me a large sea bream each for our last supper. Lynn and Susie had something off the menu as they do not like fish very much. George also told us that we will not have to be out of our room until 1 pm tomorrow so that was also very kind. This will mean that once again we can go on the beach early tomorrow morning for the last sunbathe and swim of our holiday. At about 11 am we will go up to our room and pack. Back to the meal which was quite a noisy occasion with much laughter and several alcoholic drinks. We finally went to bed at about midnight…

June 2014 in our Garden

Time to go home - Andy is waving goodbye!

Friday 13th June: We fly home on **YES** Friday the 13th but that's ok as both Susie and I are not superstitious. As already mentioned we went onto the beach between 8 am and 11 am then packed our bags (sob). Everyone we met said their fond farewells to us and said see you again next year. Troulos Bay Hotel could be likened to an Annual General Meeting (AGM) for regular patrons. After we finished packing we had a cup of tea on the balcony before going downstairs to await our fate… Dori collected our cases from outside our room and brought them down to reception for us to save my poor knees once more. We were due to leave the hotel at 3.35 pm so we had time to have lunch in the restaurant at our favourite table. This also gave us the chance to say goodbye to Ervin, Tim, Michel, Vangelis, Yannis and the family. At the appointed time the coach arrived to take us to the airport for our 7 pm Skiathos time flight home, everyone came out to see us off and this must have looked interesting to those already on the coach as they gave us quite a look when Susie and I stepped onto the coach. Arriving at the airport we went through checking in quite easily and quickly. Then we sat outside the terminal building having a smoke before going through into the departure lounge 30 minutes before lift off time.

The plane roared down the runway on time and it was time for us to bid a fond farewell to our paradise island of Skiathos until the next time…

June 2014 in our Garden

Holiday Memories!

Featuring from top left to bottom right: Dori Gardening Greek Style - Alan at Bello's - Susie at Bello's - Alan with his Walking Stick - Susie in front of the Troulos Bay Hotel…

June 2014 in our Garden

Holiday Memories!

Featuring from top left to bottom right: Alan all at Sea - Alan in sunglasses - Alan and Susie at Bello's - Susie In the Old Port Skiathos Town - Susie by our room no. 318…

June 2014 in our Garden

Holiday Memories!

Featuring from top left to bottom right: Dori in Action - Andrew (Rango Tango) and Dori after the Tennis Match - Andrew and Lynn on the beach - Susie - Ervin and Susie - Ervin the main Man…

June 2014 in our Garden

Holiday Memories!

Featuring from top left to bottom right: Floats going out to Sea - Andrew and Lynn at the Hotel pool bar - Susie in Town - Greek Cats…

June 2014 in our Garden

Holiday Memories!

Featuring from top left to bottom right: Alan all at sea - Troulos Bay Hotel at Dusk - Around Troulos Bay Hotel and Beach - Yammas to ALL our friends at Troulos Bay Hotel and all our visitor Friends - Susie and Alan…

June 2014 in our Garden

Arriving back in the UK!

Friday 13th June: We landed at Gatwick right on time 8.20 pm (UK time) and after going through passport control and baggage reclaim we walked out into the UK tired but ready to get home. We stopped off and got some milk on the way so we could have a drink. A cup of tea for me and coffee for Susie arriving home at 11.50 pm.

Back to Our Garden - Again!

We just unlocked the front door pulled our case into the lobby at the bottom of the stairs where they will remain until tomorrow. The next job was a cupper. Next we put the outside lights on so we could go outside to view the damage to our garden. We were pleased to see that although everything in the pots and beds were dry everything looked OK. On further inspection not everything was good news the grass had grown quite tall in the last two weeks, the plants in the wall baskets were all dead along with a few other plants in pots that had either bolted or shrivelled due to lack of water. We found out later that it had been very warm and sunny in the UK for the last few days hence the few plants that did not make it! Susie immediately watered the patio pots before we finished our drinks and then it was off to bed because we were very tired. It was now 1 am UK time but we were still on Skiathos time so for us it was 3 am…

June 2014 in our Garden

Up with the lark!

Saturday 14th June: Susie was up at 6 am and I followed at 7 am and after a cup of tea/coffee we were ready for the off. We started by weeding the beds then dead heading all the flowers and then moved the pots we had moved into a shady position whilst we were away back to there usual places in the sun. After two hours we had a full large bag of weeds which we then added to by removing all the casualties out of the wall baskets and two of the pots. Still not to bad only seven plants in need of replacing. Oh no! We will just have to go to a garden centre soon and get some more plants. After this it was time for a quick rest before going to the supermarket to restock our fridge, collect the cats from the cattery, unpack the cases and start the mammoth job of washing our holiday clothes. All this before we could get back to the important job of sorting our garden out and getting it back to the garden that we so love.

Bringing the boys home!

Marble and Jasper back in our garden after their holidays

June 2014 in our Garden

Bringing our garden back under control!

Sunday 15th June: We started at 9 am and by 2 pm we had tamed the garden once more and it was back under control. When we had finished we found that we had only lost the violas in the five wall baskets and three of the plants in pots so that was not to bad after all… I emptied the baskets and three pots ready to replant these up with replacement plants when we go to the garden centre tomorrow. As my right knee is still painful I will phone up the doctors tomorrow and get an emergency appointment so he can have a look at it and diagnose what needs to be done to make the pain go away.

Out and about!

Monday 16th June: I phoned the doctor at 9 am and he said I could have an appointment for 11 am that same day so that was excellent. It will be great to find out just what extra damage our holiday has done to my knee and what needs to be done to get it right. Susie would have to take me to keep the appointment so we decided to go and get some more wild bird seed and peanuts after my appointment and then go onto the garden centre to look at some replacement plants for the ones that we have lost.

Fading memories!

It is strange how quickly you start to forget your holiday and get back into the routine of being home. It is all very Sad really…

June 2014 in our Garden

The all clear!

The doctor gave my knee a thorough examination and told me that my badly twisted right knee medial ligament had not got any worse and with rest it should recover without the need of surgery… **PHEW!** We left the surgery with this good news ringing in our ears and it was then off to get the bird supplies and then onto the garden centre. We managed to get some trailing plants for our wall baskets (Petunias and Geraniums) and strangely enough we managed to find a flower plant that we had admired when we were in Skiathos. This is called Lantana and has clusters of pink, red and white tiny flowers and is very attractive. Whilst at the garden centre Susie also bought me a cordless grass strimmer as a present. This was to save my legs by not having to use the heavy mower on our front bank. So armed with these new purchases we went home to plant the new plants and assemble my new piece of equipment ready for action tomorrow.

The - me – me - me society!

We have only been home from Skiathos for just a few days but already we have noticed what a frantic society we in Briton live in. Nobody seems to have the time for anyone else in the UK any more. Many people drive like they have exclusive rights on the road, shop as if their very life depended upon it and ignore others at all cost whilst shouting down their mobile phone. This is a far cry from the people of Greece who live life at a much slower pace and are open and friendly with visitors. They always find the time for a coffee and a chat. That is why we love going to Greece as often as we can and would love to be able to afford to live on our paradise island of Skiathos **ONE DAY!**…

June 2014 in our Garden

Feeding time Again!

Tuesday 17th June: This morning we fed all of the plants in the greenhouse, beds and pots with liquid fertilizer. This will help boast the plants after being neglected for the last two weeks. This done it was time to hang the two plaques that we had bought ourselves whilst on holiday on Skiathos onto the wall in our carport:

The plaques consist of one metal sign saying "Another day in paradise" with a painted lighthouse and seascape (to remind us of our paradise island) and a ceramic disc with a stylised moon and stars on it (to remind us of our times sitting on our hotel balcony looking at the heavens) also shown is a picture of the boats in Skiathos Bay and the poster I had printed of Troulos Bay beach and put up in our carport at home! Memories are made of this!

Strimming into action!

By 12 am it was time to try out our new strimmer on the grass bank. I was looking forward to this as I have not used one before. Susie made me don a pair of safety shoes, gloves and some safety goggles before I started (we had already charged up the strimmer battery from dawn). The strimmer did a great job of the bank in reducing the overgrown grass down to a tidy finish and my knee was not put under any undue strain so thank you Susie for that. This done our garden was finally back to how it was before we left it. mission accomplished…

June 2014 in our Garden

The joy of dead heading (off with their heads he cried)!

Wednesday 18th June: Now that we have finally finished planting up our last few containers it is time to sit back for the next few months and enjoy the multitude of flowers we will undoubtedly get. However, there will still be a few regular jobs that will need to be done such as:

- The daily replenishing of the bird feeders
- Regular mowing the back lawn and strimming the front bank
- Watering the greenhouse plants daily and outside plants as and when required
- Regular feeding of all plants with liquid fertilizer

Sailing off Skiathos…

And of course there is always the daily jobs!

- The daily job of dead heading

Dead heading needs to be done every day and is one of the most important jobs a gardener can do because it stimulates the plants into putting up fresh flowers and thereby, extending their flowering season. I do this daily from early summer through to the middle of August and then I give the plants a break so that the flowers they produce from then on can be pollinated by the bees and produce their seeds as nature intended. I can say that it is for this reason only that I stop dead heading but in reality it is more selfish than that. By allowing the flowers to mature and produce seed it will also allow my seed collector (Susie) to collect their seeds in September so I can store them in envelopes inside and use them to start new life next spring thus completing the circle of life…

June 2014 in our Garden

Oliver also returns once more!

Thursday 19th June: Since we have returned from holiday we have not seen our pheasant called Oliver until this morning. He arrived for his breakfast along with all the other usual wild birds at 6.30 am and again at 4 pm for his afternoon tea. So now our garden is truly back in balance once more with not just the garden looking its best but its wild life all present and accounted for.

The last hurrah!

Today I received, by post, the last plant that I had ordered from Sutton Seeds earlier in the year. I had forgotten that I still had this to come. It was a Lonicera "Chic & Choc" honeysuckle climbing plant (dwarf). Luckily the pot containing the Lofos "Burgundy Falls" had not grown too much and there was still space to put the new plant in the middle of this pot. This also gave me the opportunity to put a plant obelisk into the pot so that both plants could use this for support and to grow up and clamber around. This really doe's complete our planting plan for this years garden **HONEST!** So after planting the new plant, watering the garden and dead heading for the day it was time to sit and watch the swallows swooping in the sky above our garden and have a cup of tea…

Swallow swooping in the sky above our garden

June 2014 in our Garden

Wedded bliss!

Friday 20th June: A date that will be forever fixed into my memory as the day I married my wonderful wife Susie. As you guessed it is our wedding anniversary today and the chance for me to celebrate another year with this fabulous woman. We exchanged gifts. I gave Susie a travel scrap book for our holiday snaps to go in, a candle, a duck ornament and some other little bits and pieces she gave me not just the strimmer (received and used earlier this week) but today she gave me all wrapped up a "Greek Eye" wind spinner and an ornament of a blue tit perched on a trowel. The Greek Eye is a traditional symbol of the Greeks and is used to ward off evil spirits. We brought one back last year from Skiathos to place just inside our front door to protect the house from evil (well you never know do you).

Susie had decided that as I seem to be accident prone in our garden it would be wise to put a Greek Eye outside to protect me from myself…

June 2014 in our Garden

World Cup exit (again - naturally)!

At 9 am today Kevin our window cleaner came. He is always happy and we often have great conversations. He has been doing our windows for several years now and he does a great job. Today however, Kevin was very sad because England had lost their second World Cup match 2-1 to Uruguay last night and after losing their first game to Italy they will be coming home early once again as usual. **How sad!** When we had discussed this at some length and he had left to continue his round and as I had taken the barrier down to let Kevin through our smoke room so he could clean the back windows I decided that the front garden still needed some work doing to bring it up to its usual standards. First job was to hoe the gravel drive to remove the numerous weeds that had sprung up in the last two weeks and then I racked the surface of the drive level. Whilst racking the drive I took some of the excess gravel in buckets and took it round to the back garden to top up the gully's in front of the patio steps, the side of the shed and in front of the greenhouse. The next job I did was to mow the back lawn before watering the plants in the front, back garden and in the greenhouse before putting the barriers back up at 1 pm.

This accomplished it was time to retire to the garden decking to soak up more sun and to have a well deserved cup of tea…

June 2014 in our Garden

The weekend break!

Saturday and Sunday 21st & 22nd June: Susie and I decided that as we had done so well it was time for some us time so we set up the decking with chairs, umbrellas, radio, sun glasses, ashtray, cigarettes, nibbles and of course a steady supply of cold drinks. We decided that we would relax and have a rest listening to BBC Radio Norfolk's Garden Party on Saturday and BBC 4 Gardeners Question Time on Sunday. I think you will all agree we have earned and deserved this weekend break.

Dulux Dogs…

Some of our blue tits are missing!

Monday 23rd June: We have noticed that since our return from holiday there has been a distinct absence of blue tits feeding on the feeders in our silver birch tree. Why this is we do not know but hope that they return shortly. So the only blue tits currently in our garden are of the ornamental kind including the one that Susie gave me for our anniversary.

The weeds are growing (again)!

Susie kindly weeded behind the back and side of our greenhouse for me as it had become overgrown with weeds that have flourished in the shade that the greenhouse provides. She also weeded the front bed at the top of our grass bank and it looked much better for it. Later she dressed it with blood, fish and bone granules to help refresh the plants growing in it. This bed is in direct sunlight for most of the day and because of this the plants were looking somewhat tired and in need of refreshment so she also watered it…

June 2014 in our Garden

It's a typical man thing!

Just like a man I have been too impatient and tried to do too much before my knee ligaments had had time to heal properly. As a result it has flared up again and it is very painful to step up and down steps again. I even had to go up to bed this evening up the stairs on my bum!

Alan resting on the patio after doing too much!

When will he ever learn!

Susie was quick to tell me off and said "I will never learn" and that "I was just like a bull in a china shop". So it's more rest for me and more workload for Susie. It is hard to be patient and wait for nature to take its course and things to improve over time with so many jobs us Gardeners have to do every day don't you agree? Thankfully I have Susie to carry me through this lack of mobility time. Still the weathers warm and dry so I will at least be able to rest outside on the patio and watch the birds feed and our flowers bloom. It is definitely a hard life but someone's got to do it…

June 2014 in our Garden

Broadening my horizons!

During my enforced rest and sitting on the patio with a few beers and with nothing but time on my hands I have had the time to reflect and marvel at all that nature has to offer. The Norfolk sky with its big horizons are helping to stimulate my own horizons and make me appreciate just how much I have gained from my gardening experiences.

The plane in our garden taking a flight

Flying display!

While I am on the subject of flying the swallows above our garden really do put on a fantastic air display. The adults have now been joined by this years babies and it is fascinating to watch the parents training their children on the finer points of feeding on the wing…

June 2014 in our Garden

Reviewing the situation (garden plant wise)!

My enforced rest has given me the opportunity to study our garden. I get a great sense of pride when I see all the wonderful flowers and fruit that we have managed to propagate and raise into strong healthy plants. All the flowers in the pots, beds and greenhouse trough are full of buds that promise a great flowering season this year with plenty of lovely blooms for Susie to cut and take indoors:

Susie who shows real skill in producing such beautiful flower arrangements for indoors from the flowers in our garden

The lemon and lime trees either side of the greenhouse door both have lots of fruit that when ripe will enhance not just our drinks but also Susie's delicious cooking. The flowers that are already in full bloom bring a multitude of colour already and will be greatly enhanced as other plants come into flower over the next few weeks…

June 2014 in our Garden

Reviewing the situation (greenhouse plant wise)!

The greenhouse is now full of strong healthy sweet pepper, tomato and cucumber plants which are now producing their first fruits. These fruit will be ready for harvesting and eating in a few weeks time.

Our new plant trough, that we made, is full of plants with flower heads coming ready for Susie to cut and take indoors and display…

June 2014 in our Garden

Plants of special merit!

As I look around me there are some plants that already deserve a special mention. First and currently foremost are the roses that are in full bloom and are looking spectacular:

The red roses are even as big as Susie's hand

June 2014 in our Garden

The other contenders!

The other plants that deserve special mention are:

1. Salvia "Ruby Neon"
2. Poppy "Californian Orange"
3. Leucanthenum "Engelina"
4. Delphinium "Black Knight"
5. Delphinium "Fox"
6. Antirrhinum "Antirinca"
7. Lavender "Ellagance"
8. Dahlia "Diablo"
9. Dahlia "Harlequin"
10. Rudbeckia "Toto"
11. Giant Fuchsia's "Bella Rosella" – "Bicentennial" – "Quasar" – "Seventh Heaven" – "Voodoo"
12. Digitalis "Iqnata Café Crème"
13. Geum "Rivale"
14. Hydrangea "Pink Delight"

Off all of the above the only plant that we have not planted in the last year is the hydrangea:

The hydrangea in full bloom is truly fantastic

June 2014 in our Garden

There be giants in our garden!

Wednesday 25th June: The five giant flowering fuchsias that we purchased as plug plants and grew on before planting up into hanging baskets are now beginning to flower:

The giant fuchsias are lovely and yes they really are very big blooms so we are in for a treat this year.

Union Jack!

Thursday 26th June: Every morning this week a young jackdaw has come into our garden to feed. He is a magnificent bird and he marches around the garden as if he owns it. We have named him, yes you have guessed it: Jack. No points there then for originality. He joins Oliver (our pheasant) and all the other wild birds in our garden that make a truly great sight for us to watch whilst we sit outside in our garden with a drink…

June 2014 in our Garden

The knock-out Blow!

Last night England drew 0 – 0 with Costa Rica to confirm that they had once again been knock out at the group stage and will be coming home early from the World Cup once more.

Shame I hear you say!

Greece on the other hand beat the Ivory Coast 2 – 1 to qualify for the knockout stages (last 16) of the World Cup for the first time in their history! The atmosphere in the bars around the Old Port of Skiathos Town must have been amazing. The Greek flag will be flying high whilst the Union Jack will be hanging limply down the flag pole.

Back to our garden!

Today the weather is sunny and warm with a temperature of 23°C so after feeding the birds, watering and dead heading it was back to the patio for tea and to read my Kindle. I am currently reading Lee Child's "The Affair" which is a great read and like most of his books, no I mean all of his books, I read them time and time again because I enjoy them so much.

The flying menace!

Friday 27th June: This morning watching the birds feed they are all too often disturbed by the flying menaces that are called pigeons. This is a real problem for the little birds but the recent arrival of Jack the jackdaw and the continued presence of Oliver the pheasant acts as a discouragement to the pigeons from coming down to feed whilst they are there…

June 2014 in our Garden

The Sports Day!

At 1 pm there was a great roar and much cheering coming from behind me as I sat on the decking. This I realised was the annual sports day. Not for me you understand (poorly knee) but for the children that attend the school just over a field behind our back garden:

This is an annual event and one that the children very much look forward too. I also look forward to hearing the cheering and encouragement given by their peers as the children take part in various races. I could not resist walking indoors and going upstairs to view this sporting spectacular for myself from our bedroom window. It was great to see the children taking part in various races over at the school and to see their enthusiasm which was only matched by the excited shouts of their parents! As the events finished and the children made their way back into school I too returned to my seating on the decking after making myself a cup of tea to await next years thrilling instalment!

Meanwhile back in our garden!

Poppy and Charlie in our garden in 2019

June 2014 in our Garden

Flying home from Rio!

The England football team flew home from Brazil today after losing two and drawing one game in the World Cup. I feel sorry for the fans that made the long and expensive trip all the way to see their fallen hero's! They would have been better advised to go to Skiathos and have a few beers in the Mythos Café Bar and watch Greece progress into the knockout stages with the locals on TV.

Back to the home front!

Having read the sad news in the paper of our hero's return from Brazil and as my knee was not too bad today I decided to mow the lawn this morning as the weather forecast for today was for heavy rain and thunder storms from tonight onwards for a few days. Oh deep joy! Norfolk is a great place to garden in because not only do you keep fit doing it (apart from the poorly knee) it also allows you to be as one with nature and you also get a sun tan into the bargain. All of the above demonstrates why **"Retiring to our Garden"** is so very beneficial on so many fronts. I am in our garden everyday, weather permitting, from 7 am until 6 pm and with an east facing garden I get the sun all day either on the patio or the decking with it finally going down behind the house at about 6.30 pm this time of the year.

The shed, the decking and the rose bed

June 2014 in our Garden

Publish or be dammed!

Saturday 28th June: Today Susie and I went to see our friends Corri and Roy. Corri has started to garden more and has already made herself a new rockery in which she has planted some lovely plants. Lucky things their hazelnut tree in their garden is amass with nuts (I think these are called Cobs) and they will make great eating when they are ready. She said that her new found gardening exploits are as a result of getting inspired when editing my first book **"Retiring to the Garden – Year One"** for me. That was a very kind thing to say and to think that I may have inspired her in some small way to garden more fills me with pride. Having viewed the garden Roy and I went to his office so I could see what progress he has made in editing my first book ready for publishing. Roy has done a great job and has already produced a front and back cover for the paperback book and improved the layout and quality of the illustrations dramatically. There is still a lot to do to get it ready for publishing but we did agree on the final formatting of the text and the position of the illustrations throughout the paperback book. This done we discussed the distribution, retail price, wholesale cost and the apportionment of profits made from both the E-book and the paperback book. The paper book and E-book should be available middle too late July and I will get 36 copies of the paperback book to give as presents to friends and family.

After this we had lunch with Corri and Roy before they returned home leaving me very happy man. Today I am a much sadder person knowing that my friend Roy is no longer with us. He died in November 2018. I owe him a vast debt of gratitude for the help, support and encouragement that he gave me when I started to write and for publishing my first two books!…

June 2014 in our Garden

Bath time in our garden!

Sunday 29th June: The pair of blackbirds that use our garden to forage for food to feed their young everyday can often be seen having a bath in our bird water bowl:

The male blackbird has a bath in our bird water bowl at least three times a day. He is such a hard worker and it is good to see him taking such good care of his personnel hygiene.

Latest washing facilities improvements in our house!

Above we see pictures of our new wet room installed in June 2018

June 2014 in our Garden

Dahlia delight!

Last year I dug up the dahlia tubers after they had finished flowering in the autumn pruned, cleaned and stored them in the shed over winter. This spring I retrieved them from the shed and planted them into four pots in the front garden. Just look at them now:

The dahlias are all "Diablo" which comes in a wide range of colours

June 2014 in our Garden

I still want more!

I know I said that we had finished buying plants for our garden this year **BUT!** Today we woke up to clear blue skies, full sun and 23°C so as one of the new plants that we had planted into one of our wall baskets had died we decided to go and see if the garden centre had any plants left. We managed to get the following (not again I hear you shout):

- 50 Acidanthera "Peacock Orchid" bulbs
- Chrysanthemum "Golden Alex"
- Chrysanthemum "Bright Eye"
- Chrysanthemum "Habenburg"
- Chrysanthemum "Beppie Bronze"
- Leucanthemum "Snow Lady"
- Fuchsia "Southgate"
- Osteospermum "Sunny Mary"
- Felicia "Feliatara"

I thought you said ONE! I hear you shout. But we did manage to find enough room for all of the above in our garden so we must have needed them!

Grow your own!

Red poppies…

Monday 30th June: We must have saved a small fortune by growing our own fruit and flowers from seed and/or taking cuttings and/or digging up dahlias and then re-planting them this year. This said I have still managed to buy several plants from garden centres this year (more than a few actually) but because of the success of growing my own new plants this year (and last year) I feel that this has offset the cost that we would have spent somewhat! I intend to extend my growing of plants from seeds and cuttings even more next year…

June 2014 in our Garden

Who's Keeping score!

As I sat on the decking resting **YES** my poor knee is still very painful. I got to thinking about just how many of this years plants I have been responsible for raising myself? I just could not resist getting up and hobbling around doing a quick tally (a bit of exercise must be good for my knee after all) only to find:

From: Zero to 360!

In the greenhouse I have raised the following plants from seed/cuttings: 7 tomato plants from seed - 2 cucumber plants from seed - 3 sweet pepper plants from seed - 8 fuchsia from cuttings - 145 flower plants from seed.

In pots I had propagated the following number of plants: 42 flower plants from cuttings - 3 flower plants from seed.

In the front and back beds I had propagated: 86 flower plants from cuttings - 64 flower plants from seed.

Total plants propagated for our garden this year to = 360!

Sitting down to add my quick five bar gate adding up method to find such a large total made me very proud of just how far I have progressed my gardening skills in the last twelve months. Next year I hope to produce about 80% of all of the plants I use in the beds, borders, baskets, pots and greenhouse myself. Wish me luck…

June 2014 in our Garden

Some of the flowers that are growing in our garden right now from top left to bottom right: Salvia, Penstemon, Petunia, Foxglove and Lavender

July 2014 in our Garden

Another one bites the dust!

Tuesday 1st July: Another month has passed in our garden and the flowers are now in the full bloom of summer. This means that I now have more time to sit and enjoy their colour and beauty with a welcome cold drink which for me has to be:

Cuba Libre time!

My preferred drink is the original cocktail of freedom. It is the drink that celebrated Cuba's independence from Spain and consists of Bacardi (white rum), cola and lime. It originated when an American soldier toasted "por Cuba Libre" with the above drink and the iconic cocktail was born. This is my favourite drink whilst sitting on the decking in the sunshine. Imagine my joy when for the first time I was able to use my very own home grown lime to make this iconic drink to welcome in the new month of July into our garden… **Cheers**!

Susie, foxes and a cat all relaxing in their own way!

July 2014 in our Garden

New life!

Wednesday 2nd July: Whilst sitting having coffee in our smoke room over the last few weeks I have noticed a pair of collar doves flying in and out of the elder tree in next doors garden with twigs in their beaks. This was obviously to build a nest and sure enough this was confirmed this morning when I saw two baby collar doves on the edge of the tree canopy being feed by one of the adults. Later the young birds flapped their wings for a while before retiring back to the safety of their nest. By **"Retiring to our Garden"** I now have the time to observe these wonders of nature and to see new life emerge. No doubt they will be fledged in the next few days.

Death comes on swift wings!

By way of contrast in the afternoon I was relaxing on the patio when I heard a great commotion in our silver birch tree. As I watched a kestrel emerged from the branches clutching a sparrow in its talons. So death had come to the garden on swift wings. Again I marvelled at the circle of life that surrounds us all every day but few have the time to witness…

Jasper watching the birds in our garden, an upside down cat and a bluebird

July 2014 in our Garden

Another day in paradise!

Thursday 3rd July: Today after finishing the usual garden tasks I had time to relax on the patio and reflect on how lucky I was because I have not just one but two paradises in my life. The first is in Troulos Bay on Skiathos and the second is our garden. Both are beautiful, tranquil and are lovely place to relax in!

The Affair!

Today I finished reading "The Affair" by Lee Child on my Kindle and I think it is definitely one of his best yet…

First flight!

The two baby collar doves took their first flight today. I have named them Anna and Issy after two good friends of ours. They flew around the tree their nest was in and then landed on our fence panel for several minutes before flying back to the safety of their nest.

The young Doves

July 2014 in our Garden

News flash: Prompt action saves the day!

Friday 4th July: Yesterday I noticed that the bacopa "Golden Leaf" plant that is in one of the hanging container on the fence near the arbour was looking very sad and almost dead. Taking immediate action I took it down and gave it a good soaking and left the pot on the gravel overnight. This morning it had not only fully recovered but had small white flowers blooming all over it. I will keep the container down until the weekend before putting it back up on the fence making sure that I water it regularly from now on.

The stars have come out!

Saturday 5th July: The Isotoma "Star-shine Blue" that I planted in the clematis pot next to the arbour came in to full bloom today and is looking spectacular.

Taking the dogs to Snettisham beach in 2019!

Our dogs Charlie and Poppy like nothing better than a run on the beach

July 2014 in our Garden

Myrtle is in bloom!

The Myrtle "Glamleam Gold" that is planted in a pot in front of the greenhouse is now in full bloom and looks very pretty.

It's Mamma Mia time!

The Mamma Mia rose that I planted into Susie's bed, near our shed; earlier this year has now come into bloom and is really beautiful and smells divine:

The name "Mamma Mia" is a reminder to us of our paradise island of Skiathos where the film of the same name was partly filmed…

July 2014 in our Garden

Getting kited up!

The weather this week has been sunny and warm between 20°C and 25°C so it's time to put my knee support on and cut the grass. This done it was back to the decking to rest my painful knee with a few glasses of Cuba Libra for good measure and watch the thrush!

The magnificent seven:

Monday 7th July: No not the cowboy film of the same name but my seven favourite flowers in this year's garden. Although all of our flowers are beautiful these are in my view the magnificent seven:

1. Salvia "Ruby Neon"
2. Poppy "Californian Orange"
3. Dahlia "Harlequin"
4. Isotoma "Starshine Blue"
5. Fuchsia "Thalia"
6. Delphinium "Fox"
7. Rudbeckia "Toto"

Other flowers of note this year are:

- Nemesia "Rose Pink"
- Dahlia "Diablo"
- Rose "Sentimental"
- Delphinium "Black Knight"
- Antirrhinum "Antirinca Rose"
- Myrtle "Glamleam Gold"
- Marigold "Wild Orange"
- Dahlia "Bishop of LLandoff"
- Begonia "Pink Flamingo"

Although too many to list all of the dahlias and fuchsias individually all are magnificent and are worthy of a separate mention if I had the space!...

July 2014 in our Garden

HOLD the front page!

Tuesday 8th July: My publisher Roy phoned me this afternoon to say that he has encountered a major problem preparing my first book for publication!

Oh NO!!!

The PDF "technical term" required for printing a high quality colour book crashed when he tried to convert my document (book) ready for the printers. Roy has spoken to an associate of his and will now use a different desk top publishing programme to hopefully produce a file that will convert successfully to a PDF format suitable for printing! I will have to wait with baited breathe to hear if he has been successful. I will let you know how he gets on later in this book.

Meanwhile Jasper does not seem too concern about the fate of my first book…

July 2014 in our Garden

The sweet smell of honey!

Wednesday 9th July: The honeysuckle that cascades over our fence that hides our central heating oil tank from view in our back garden is now in full bloom. When you walk passed it you get this delicious smell of honey. The honeysuckle was already there when we moved into our house/garden so that was lucky. We have added a sweet smelling jasmine to grow through it. The jasmine has small pink flowers and the honeysuckle has yellow and white flowers so they make a striking combination.

Warning!

A word of warning these two plants are very vigorous and grow very quickly and soon can get out of control if left to their own devises. If left unchecked they can soon take over your garden so regular pruning is essential.

Lazy day in our garden!

Laying and Landing in our garden

July 2014 in our Garden

Pruning without fear!

I use a cordless hedge trimmer for keeping the honeysuckle and jasmine in check or should I say Susie climbs on top of our oil tank to cut them back (my poorly knee you know).

Susie clearing up the honeysuckle cuttings with Marble looking on!

We find this is the best way (note the Royal use of we) to keep these climbing plants in check and by using a cordless hedge trimmer means there are no pesky electric cable to cut through. We use cordless electrical equipment for all of our outdoor jobs such as drilling, strimming and trimming it is much safer.

Old Boy's resting in our garden

July 2014 in our Garden

BUT… be careful out there!

A word of warning to all would be hedge trimmers out there remember too engage brain before letting yourself or others lose on your prized hedge. You could, like me, end up murdering it! For those of you that have not read, as yet, my first book **"Retiring to the garden – Year 1"** (why not?) my wife Susie contacted the BBC Radio Norfolk Garden Party experts asking them why our hedge had developed big ugly brown patches all over it? They told us that I had cut it to an inch of its life and had in fact "murdered" it… They recommended that we plant evergreen clematis in front of these brown patches and that over time these will climb up and hide the offending areas.

Murder up-date!

We planted eight clematis and six climbing evergreen ivy as directed last year and this has been a great success because they have already covered most of the brown patches and some have even reached the top of the hedge.

Another major benefit of doing this is that earlier this year many of the clematis flowered for the first time and were beautiful. This can only get better in the years ahead so I thank the experts on BBC Radio Norfolk The Garden Party for turning my over zealous hedge trimming into a success story however, **remember unlike me do not murder your hedge first! …**

July 2014 in our Garden

The bells are ringing for me and my girl!

Thursday 10th July: For the last few weeks it has been mainly clear blue sky and warm sun every day with temperatures between 20°C and 25°C. It has therefore, become our habit that when Susie gets home from work during the week we spend the early evening sitting on the decking with our gin and tonic or in my case Cuba Libra. On a Thursday this routine is further enhanced by the bell ringers of our village church practicing session at 7 pm. So we sit and listen to the bells whilst watching the swallows darting and swooping in the sky above us with ok an occasional sip of our drinks.

The call of the wild!

Friday 11th July: Every weekday morning between 6 am and 7 am we sit in our smoke room enjoying a coffee before Susie leaves for work. We will be enjoying this early morning quite period when all of a sudden we will hear the call of the wild animals and birds that are all around us!…

July 2014 in our Garden

The boy arrives!

To be more specific it will be Oliver the pheasant strutting towards the smoke room asking for his breakfast. He is now getting very tame around us and stands next to you while you fill his feeding bowl out on the lawn. He even has the good manners of thanking you for his food with a loud cluck! Jack the jackdaw is also a regular visitor to our garden each day for his breakfast and afternoon brunch!

Time to reflect!

After feeding the birds (Oliver and Jack included) I continue to sit either in the smoke room or move onto the patio after Susie leaves for work for another hour or so before starting the daily tasks of watering and dead heading. During this relaxation time I cannot help admire our superb fuchsias:

I love these flowers because they remind me of when I use to spend my summer school holidays staying with my Uncle Frank, Aunty Joyce and their daughter Beryl in the small North Norfolk village of North Creake where Uncle Frank would grow lots of fuchsias in pots…

July 2014 in our Garden

When I was a boy (a very long, long, long time ago)!

Frank had lots of vegetables growing in his garden and would line his back path and around his shed with standard fuchsias which looked superb. Whilst I am thinking about my memories of when I was a boy I remember that it was whilst staying in North Creake that I developed my love of dahlias:

Alan then and now…

When staying with my aunty and uncle I would sometimes go and help an old lady gather dahlias from her front garden ready to band into bunches to sell from a little stall by her front gate. It is amazing how much of what we are now comes from the experiences that we had as a child…

July 2014 in our Garden

My gardening heroes!

Olivia gardening…

Whilst sipping tea/coffee on my patio to rest my poorly knee I turned my mind too people who I owe a debt of gratitude for my love and appreciation of gardening. So I have already written about Uncle Frank, the Old Lady already but I should also mention the provider of my "Magic Power" Mrs Smith who I helped take carnation cuttings (lots) who gave me a tub of hormone rooting powder that she gave the creative name to and set me on my way to successful propagation. I thank them ALL! Interestingly these gardening heroes of mine all influenced me when I was a boy and their influence has live on all these years even though they have all since died… **BUT** that is not the case with my last garden hero he is still very much alive and gardens everyday even though he is over eighty years of age! Who then is he? Well my big sister Phyllis use to invite me to hers for a meal or even for a weeks holiday when I was a teenager. Invariably when I arrived at her house her husband Dennis would usually be out in the garden tending his vegetable plot. I can remember being well impressed (but to cool to say so) by how neat and tidy his garden always was and just how much he had managed to sow from seeds that had developed into wonderful vegetables. He always said "good gardening is almost entirely down to good planning and preparation of the soil". I now know that he was so right and I try to practice what he preached and am only sorry that I could not tell him at the time how great I thought his garden was (the vagaries of youth). But I can now: **Thank you Dennis.** It is strange to think just how much of who we are comes from often unrecognised events and that is why I have fond memories of when I was young…

July 2014 in our Garden

A star is born!

Saturday 12th July: Roy my publisher has managed to finalise the PDF of my first book and it is now ready to go off to the printers to produce my book in paperback. He will then arrange for it to be distributed world wide on Internet site's such as Amazon. He will also put my book on as an E-BOOK on the same sites. I will then officially be an author. Deep joy! I will paint and frame a painting just for Roy and also give him a bottle of champagne when he brings me my paperbacks to say thank you. What can I say other than: **Roy you are my STAR!**

Roy's painting…

The calm after the storm!

Sunday 13th July: After what was for me yesterdays historic news Susie and I cracked open a bottle of champagne to celebrate my forthcoming book whilst sitting in our beloved garden.

Roy I raise my glass to you and now it is back to the gardening as we both chanted "Ding, Dong the book is done"!…

July 2014 in our Garden

A new gardening disciple is born!

Roy has told me that Corri, since she proof read my first book, has decided to spend more time in her garden gardening. She has already built herself a new rockery and is learning the names of the existing plants in her garden. She is also adding more plants to her garden.

A new gardener is born!

All of the above is fantastic news and it just keeps getting better as she is now taking pictures of her garden and keeping a notebook relating to her gardening adventures. She has even found the time too produce her own book about her garden. Talking to her husband Roy it would appear that he is even taking a greater interest in all things gardening. We had a long chat about him getting a cold frame for Corri to propagate her own new plant cuttings in.

First Edition…

2nd Edition…

To think that my book has played just a small part in getting them inspired to garden more is wonderful and I wish them every success in their garden in the future. In 2019 I did a second edition of this very book!…

July 2014 in our Garden

Feed me Mum (or Dad)!

Monday 14th July: The family of blackbirds are now coming into our garden so the adults can feed their young on the ground (1 first hatchling – 2 second hatchlings). They make quite a show.

Above we see the male blackbird showing the young how to take a bath. The young flap their wings very fast to get the adults to feed them. The strange thing is that all of the young are bigger than their parents! My knee feels much better today so I have cut the lawn and watered the greenhouse, pots and beds.

The first of our garden harvest!

Today I harvested a home grown lemon from our fruit tree. The lemon Susie used in her cookery that same day. She made a fish pie topped with pastry and she told me that she used the squeezed lemon juice in the sauce that went in with the fish. Lovely grubbily…

July 2014 in our Garden

I'm on the road again!

Tuesday 15th July: As my knee has been much better of late I decided to go and get my haircut in Downham Market this morning:

This is the first time I have driven my car in more than ten weeks. It started first time! After returning from my trip out at 10.30 am my knee was a bit painful so I decided to go and relax on the decking and read my kindle for the rest of the day. Oh it is such a hard life!

Beware danger!

It is ridiculous to think that I damaged my right knee by just stepping out of the greenhouse. So although I would recommend the merits of you getting your hands dirty in your garden I must from practical experience tell you too beware it is dangerous out there and that you must (including me) engage your brain at all times. Remember simple activities can be the most dangerous but such are the hazards of being a gardener…

July 2014 in our Garden

My Knee needs a rest!

Wednesday 16th July: After yesterday's car trip adventure I will spend today doing nothing much at all in the hope that a good days rest might help reduce the pain somewhat.

Mamma Mia time!

Thursday 17th July: Today I noticed that the rose "Mamma Mia" is now in full bloom:

Whilst I was trying to rest my poorly knee as much as possible I still had to top up the bird feeders, water the plants but with the weather being blue skies, white fluffy clouds and temperatures reaching 28°C I took plenty of rest breaks for relaxing on the decking.

Oh happy days!

Even the little people are happy in our garden!

July 2014 in our Garden

Peacocks on the Buddleja bush or the Butterfly bush!

Friday 18th July: Our butterfly bush is covered with peacock butterflies and makes a tremendous sight:

It's official!

I am a published author: at about 11 am today Roy came round with a box of my first paperback book. They looked great and I thanked Roy and gave him the watercolour painting that I had painted and framed just for him (he will put it on his study wall hopefully). I also gave Roy a bottle of champagne to have back home with Corri to celebrate our joint success! I proudly placed a copy of my book and two champagne flutes (empty) on the dinning room table to await Susie's return from work at about 5.30 pm. We can then toast the success of my latest adventure…

July 2014 in our Garden

Getting ready to pop the cork!

I spent the time pre-celebration by cutting the lawn, feeding the birds and dead heading the flowers such are the joys of being a published garden author! The temperature was 30°C when Susie got home from work at 5.45 pm so flutes in hand we went to celebrated by taking our bottle of bubbly outside to toast our garden and my book from the comfort of the decking recliners. This was a very happy end to a very successful day.

Bang – Bang!

Saturday 19th July: We were rudely woken up this morning at 4.30 am by a big clap of thunder and the bedroom was lit up with flashes of lightning. So worrying about our cats we got up and went outside to the smoke room for a coffee and to allow the cats to rush inside because they were scared. Having sat there for an hour we decided to go early and do our weekly shop at the supermarket as they opened 24 hours a day. We arrived back from our shopping expedition and Susie had put it all way by 9 am. **WOW!**

We had another coffee this time on the patio as the storm had passed and it was now sunny and 25°C. Whilst enjoying our break we noticed that the blue tits so long missing from our bird feeders had once again returned. I do not know where they had been but it was great to see them back again…

July 2014 in our Garden

The Pony Express or Wells Fargo or even Royal Mail!

Having received my paperback books yesterday from Roy and after buying some padded envelopes whilst out shopping today we decided to post off two of my books to our friends Alistair and Issy in Scotland and Karl and Anna in Vienna Austria. Susie took these down to the Post Office to post for me at 10 am. Our friends Andrew, Lynn and their dog Franky will be visiting us for a few days on the 9th August so we decided to keep their copy of my book here and give it to them then.

Andy, Lynn, Franky and Baz…

The other books I will give as gifts when we either see other friends and family or give them as Christmas presents. I will take our friends in Skiathos a copy next year when we go once more to our paradise island. Today I also finished my second notebook for this year so tomorrow I will start number three. Last year I only used one notebook for the whole year so either I have had more things to write about this year or I have really got into this note taking lark…

July 2014 in our Garden

Sharpening up my pencil!

Sunday 20th July: A new day and a new notebook so pencil sharpened ready to go its back to the garden. People say that gardening is a hobby but it is not it is more a way of life. That said my garden for me meant that:

I've found my marbles (they were just a click away)!

No not our cat marbles but my marbles. Not the round glass sort that I played with when I was young although I still have those in a bag upstairs but rather the way to keep my brain ticking over in my old age namely my art work, my gardening but most of all what you see here… Yes the written word. One click and it's there! I have found that by recording the events and adventures I have had in our garden that as well as enjoying the act of gardening and painting I now enjoy writing about it just as much. This has come as quite a shock to me because anyone who knows me would not say that I had any written skills whatsoever. None the less I have found that even though I can not spell; find it hard to put more than two sentences together and my grammar is appalling the act of getting into the habit of writing daily has been both rewarding and has helped to keep the old grey matter ticking over!

Back to our garden!

Sliding my orange box firmly back under the dining room table it is now time to get into our garden and practice what I have been preaching. Feeding, weeding, watering, mowing, dead heading and generally having great fun…

July 2014 in our Garden

More supplies!

After I had completed the daily gardening tasks it was off shopping (Susie drove) to get some more wild bird food. While out we called into a local garden centre and yes you know what comes next… More plants:

- 6 dahlia red collection tubers for next year's garden. These included "Cactus Berger's Record" – "Mignon Firebird" – "Garden Wonder" – "Little Tiger" – "Nescio"
- Begonia "White Beauty"
- Geranium "Yellow Jewel"
- Nemesia "Purple Pride"
- Cape Marigold "Rain Daisy"
- Cosmos "Chocomocha"

These we took home and put the tubers upstairs for next year and planted the rest of the plants into spare pots. I will over winter these pots in the greenhouse ready for planting into beds/pots next season.

The Hard worker!

Monday 21st July: Yesterday when we got home from our shopping expedition Susie carried in the things from the car for me to save my poorly knee. Some people might say that she has become a slave to my mobility problem!

Some more of our garden flowers

July 2014 in our Garden

Let's do it again!

Tuesday 22nd July: While sipping my morning cup of tea I could not help but marvel at the profusion of colour provided by the dahlias and fuchsias all around our garden. To think that now I know how to successfully over winter dahlia tubers and successfully take fuchsia cuttings I can now reproduce the same effect next year and for many more years to come (I hope).

Lowering the barriers!

Wednesday 23rd July: This morning bright and early I took down the wooden slats that make up our barrier between the front garden and the smoke room. This was to enable me to clean my car ready for it's MOT tomorrow morning. The second reason for taking the barriers down was to allow access for our window cleaner Kevin so he could clean our back house windows later on today. After cleaning the car I used my hedge trimmer to take the top 20 cm off the front bank bed salvias to encourage new flower stems to form and then flower. Having done all this and finding that I could still walk I cut the front bank grass whilst waiting for Kevin to come. He came at 3 pm and I put the barriers back up after he left at 3.50 pm.

NO MORE! - Lowering the barriers!

The side gate that I made in 2018…

In 2018 I fixed the wooden barriers permanently in place and put a side gate in so I no longer had to raise the barriers!

July 2014 in our Garden

The MOT!

Thursday 24th July: Before I set off this morning at 7.30 am to get my Vauxhall Zafira MOT done I saw a greater spotted woodpecker on our bird feeder in the back garden. I took this as a good sign and was proved right as once again my car passed its MOT first time with no work required. I have been taking my car to Thurlow Nunn of Kings Lynn for the last six years for my car MOT with always the same outcome. Great!

My pain goes on and on!

Friday 25th July: Today my right knee is very painful once more which is probably due to yesterdays driving but I still had jobs to do in the garden. The lawn needed mowing and as it is 28°C today I needed to water everything as well so when I completed these tasks and fed the birds I retreated to the patio to rest and recover I hope. As this knee problem has been going on for nearly three months I will be going back to my doctors to see what can be done to speed the recovery of my medial ligament.

Time to rest (again)!

Norfolk poppy field…

Saturday 26th July: Today was a really lovely day with temperatures reaching 28°C as it has done all week so after completing the usual jobs Susie and I retired to the decking for the rest of the day. We listened to the BBC Radio Norfolk Garden Party and had a few drinks and dreamed of fields of poppies!

Feeding time!

Sunday 27th July: Today Susie and I fed all the plants with liquid fertilizer. This included all of the plants in our pots, borders and in the greenhouse…

July 2014 in our Garden

The grim reaper!

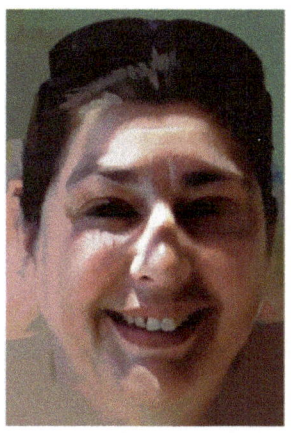 

Susie decided to not only weed all of the beds after we fed all of the plants but she also decided to remove all of the early spent flowers in the beds. These included dead or dying foxgloves, Russell Lupins, delphiniums and aquilegia. This action by my very own grim reaper had created several gaps in our beds that she then proceeded to fill with flowering pots of plants from the patio and elsewhere. When I asked her why she had done this she said "it will be just like they do at the Chelsea Flower Show". I must admit that when she had finished the beds looked quite full again so well done Susie!

Bee and Butterfly heaven!

Monday 28th July: It rained heavily first thing this morning but by mid-morning the sun was out again and it was 23°C so all of the bees and butterflies were back on our lavender, rudbeckia, dahlias and buddleja once more as they have been for many weeks. This is wonderful to see and makes all the planting, nurturing and dead heading worthwhile.

Payback time - Well not really!

We get all the bees and butterflies in our garden because we provide them with the food supply that they want and of course the warm sunny weather that is needed for the flowers to bloom well is provided for us hopefully. The hard work that Susie and I have put into our garden again this year has been well worth it because we have been repaid many times over by the wild life, fruit, and flowers that our garden has given us in return…

July 2014 in our Garden

Moving towards a crescendo!

Tuesday 29th to Thursday 31st July: As we reach a crescendo of colour in our garden I have spent the last three days of this month not only doing all the usual daily tasks but have been taking pictures of some of the best blooms in our garden. These are below:

Top left to bottom middle: Antirrhinum Rose, Cornflower and pots of Dahlia's

August 2014 in our Garden

Using the can!

Friday 1st August: Sometimes I have to use the watering can on flowers that are too delicate for watering with the hose pipe so today I watered these plants with my fine headed watering can:

This done I turned my attention to the coal storage bunker that we made a few years ago. Over time the plastic that we had covered it with had become torn and brittle so the bunker was no longer water proof. It was now time to re-cover this so it would once again be water tight before the winter sets in. To do this we are going to utilise some wood effect vinyl that we had saved when we replaced this with carpet in our front entrance porch. I measured and cut the vinyl into pieces to fit the bunker and tomorrow Susie will help me fit these into place on the coal bunker…

August 2014 in our Garden

Cladding the bunker!

Saturday 2nd August: Susie and I clad the bunker with the vinyl this morning and after we finished Susie raked the gravel level so we could placed the bunker back in the corner of our smoke room. Susie then refilled it with bags of smokeless coal ready for the coming winter. It looked much better clad in the vinyl and should be very affective at keeping the rain out for a few more years. Susie then went off to do our weekly shop and returned with a present for me. She presented me with a new garden sign that said "Alan's Garden – Genius at Work" which I thought was very apt. I screwed this straight up on to the top inside back of the arbour for all to admire.

Gathering all the colours of the rainbow!

Sunday 3rd August: This morning Susie gathered some more cut flowers for the house:

One vase she put onto our dinning room table and displayed a copy of my new book beside it. The flowers looked great as did the book…

August 2014 in our Garden

Not long now!

Monday 4th August: This morning I went to see the Doctor for a review of my poorly right knee. He was pleased with its progress and said that I should be pain free in about two weeks but I would still need to be careful with it for another three months. This was good news so I went home and sat in the garden before carefully watering and deadheading the flowers and greenhouse plants. Sitting on the patio afterwards I admired our perfusion of flowers and in particularly the marigolds that were looking fabulous.

Our house Front In 2019…

Sleepy boy…

There be dragons!

Tuesday 5th August: While reading on the patio this morning I became aware of a high pitched noise. Looking up I spotted two dragon flies hovering over the dahlias in pots at the front of our patio wall. This is truly one of nature's true marvels and one that man has been able to witnessing since mankind first appeared on earth…

August 2014 in our Garden

Up the steps!

Wednesday 6th August: My right knee continues to improve and I am now able to walk further with less pain. I am trying to be careful not to undo all these last weeks of inactivity by avoiding carrying stuff or climbing steps or twisting my knee whenever possible. So when I want to go onto the back lawn I use the slight sloop beside the patio instead of going up the steps that lead from the patio to the lawn.

Pots up the patio steps and Susie, Mum and Bailey in our garden in 2019

August 2014 in our Garden

Goodbye to another old friend!

Thursday 7th August: Today our cat Jasper died. He has been gradually fading away for some time. He was 16 years of age. We will miss him greatly as we still do his brother Dusty who died last November.

This sad event was made even worse because today was the first day of Susie's week long holiday from work so not a good first day!

New life!

In memory of Jasper we decided to help create some new life today. We composted four large 3 litre pots and using magic powder took 24 cuttings of fuchsia "Thalia", salvia "Ruby Neon", Olive, Bay and Lantana "Skiathos Memories" and planted these into our filled pot edges. It was a help to us to create new life after the loss of Jasper. We must keep an extra eye on Marble because he has never been the only cat before…

August 2014 in our Garden

Franky comes to Town (our garden)!

Saturday 9th August: Today our friends from holiday Andrew and Lynn are bring their dog Franky to stay with us for a few days:

Harvest time!

Today we also harvested our first tomato fruit from the greenhouse so we will be able to use these in our salads to entertain our friends (not Franky as he prefers meat not fruit). Andrew and Lynn also came bearing gifts for us: a lovely Calla plant for Susie and a bottle of Bacardi and lots of bottled beer for me. We gave them a copy of my first book and three framed pictures of them on holiday on Skiathos that we had taken this year.

The boys are back!

To complete the day the two collar doves that I watched taking their first flights are now feeding in our garden daily and they still spend some time sitting on our fence each morning…

August 2014 in our Garden

Walking the dog!

Sunday 10th August: The weather this weekend is not very good with lots of rain and strong winds so apart from taking Franky for a walk at a local dog walking woodland we stayed at home today.

All blown up!

Monday 11th August: I woke up this morning to find that the whole left hand side of my face had swollen up overnight. I phoned the dentist who fitted me in today at 1.30 pm so whilst I stayed at home in the morning Susie, Andrew, Lynn and Franky went for a seaside walk at a beach near us. They came home at 1 pm to take me to get my face sorted out at Downham Market. The dentist gave me a week's treatment of penicillin and I will have to go back next Wednesday to have a tooth taken out. **Ouch!**

Breakfast on the patio!

Tuesday 12th August: Today Andrew, Lynn and Franky are going home to Sheffield but before they went we were able to have a three hour breakfast on the patio as the weather had improved considerably.

They left at about 2 pm and we will miss them as they were such good company and Franky was amazing…

August 2014 in our Garden

A cunning plan!

We both said after our guests had gone how much we had enjoyed their company and how Franky had reminded us of when we had had our dogs Polly and Megan they were both Cavalier Kings Charles. Susie must have had a cunning plan for later that same evening she showed me some pictures of some adorable puppies (a breed called Cavapoo). We decided that as their owners only live a few miles from us we would perhaps go and have a look at them tomorrow.

Decision time!

We set off to look at the puppies and liked them so much we decided to get not one but two new pets. They are just over seven weeks old. One is a black and white female and the other is a black male. We will be collecting them on Saturday 23rd August after they have had their first injection. We decided to call them Poppy for the female and Charlie for the male. They are a brother and sister act:

Poppy and Charlie

On the way home we stopped at a store called Bearts' and bought a pair of dog baskets, cushions, leads, collars, chews and dog food ready for when the puppies come home…

August 2014 in our Garden

Preparing the way!

Thursday 14th August: As we had a few days before the puppies would be home we set about making a run, dog gate and generally improving the garden boundary fencing to hopefully safely contain the little ones.

Back to our garden!

Friday 15th August: Having done what we could to improve our dog retaining defences it was time for me to spend some time focusing on the garden once more. I set about cutting the lawn, dead heading and watering to keep the garden as good as I can keep it!

Charlie and Poppy indoors in 2019 and Susie and Alan on holiday on Skiathos in 2014

August 2014 in our Garden

Dog tags!

Saturday 16th August: This morning whilst shopping we got Poppy and Charlie a dog tag each with their names on and our phone number just in case!

More plants!

It was not just dog tags that we got we also found some more plants for our garden (I hope they do not get dug up). We got: Liatris "Specata Alba" and Primula "Vialli". These we planted when we got home then we continued to improve our perimeter fencing ready for our new pets.

The hedge cutter!

Sunday 17th August: Today after we had nipped out to get some more fat balls and peanuts for the birds I charged up my hedge trimmer ready to cut back some sage "Hot Lips" and the hedge beside our bin storage area because I am getting fed up with getting wet when putting stuff into the bins… This done and with the weather again getting cold and wet we went inside for our first Sunday roast for many a month!

Marble has been very quite since Jasper died so we hope he will rally around when the dogs arrive…

August 2014 in our Garden

Flowers galore!

Monday 18th – Friday 22nd August: Some of the many colourful flowers in our garden currently flowering:

Top left to bottom right: Dahlia, Sunflower, Leucanthemum and Helanium. More pictures of our garden flowers to come later in the month…

August 2014 in our Garden

A fine pair of tails!

Saturday 23rd August: Today we collected our new puppies Poppy (female black and white) and Charlie (Male black with white chin) at 10.30 am. They are eight weeks old and full of energy. We took the dog breeder some of our ripe tomatoes that we grew from seed as we have a bumper crop at present.

Top of the league at Portman Road!

Norwich City FC played their fourth game of the season at Ipswich today and won 1 – 0. They have now won three matches this session and are top of the league. Let's hope they are still there at the end of the season and get back into the Premiership were we belong!

Puppy update!

Sunday 24th August: Poppy and Charlie slept all night only waking when Susie went down in the morning at 6 pm. This was a very good start.

Coating the shed!

Today Susie and I also found the time to re-treat the garden shed with Willow wood preserver whilst the dogs slept on the patio. This took us from 9 am to 1 pm to achieve so we joined the puppies when we were finished for drinks. I had a Cuba Libra and Susie had a glass of wine and the dogs had water…

August 2014 in our Garden

A very good boy and girl!

Monday 25th August: Poppy and Charlie were great again last night and after playing with them for a while we decided to leave them in their pen indoors at 9.50 am and go shopping for more dog food, biscuits and toys returning home at 12.10 pm. All was quite so that was another success. It rained hard all day so it was hard to amuse the puppies and we were all very tired by the end of the day.

It will be time for a jab soon!

Tuesday 26th August: The puppies slept all night again last night and after playing for an hour they settled down to sleep. This is when I done the dirty deed! I phoned up the Crossings Veterinary Centre to book the puppies in for their second injection. They were born on the 24.06.2014. I booked to take them for their jab on Wednesday 3rd September at 4.25 pm. Charlie and Poppy are settling in well, eating well and today they were very well behaved indeed.

Poppy and Charlie feasting and on the lawn with Susie in 2014 and the trough we made now living in our front garden in 2019 with flowers in…

August 2014 in our Garden

Back to our Garden!

Wednesday 26th – Saturday 30th August: Pictures from around the garden in 2019 and our visitors in 2014!

Guests for lunch!

Sunday 31st August: Last day of the month and Corri and Roy came to see the new puppies today. The dogs were very good. We had lunch and afterwards I demonstrated to Corri how to take cuttings from fuchsias and salvias. She took some potted cuttings home and I look forward to seeing them in her garden next year. As already mentioned sadly Roy is no longer with us and is sadly missed!…

September 2014 in our Garden

A change of tack!

Monday 1st September: Another month passes and a new one begins so I have decided that for the rest of this book I will not use my computer software programme to manipulate my photographs and will put them in unaltered for the months ahead however, I will still scan in any watercolour paintings that I do and paste these in to the pages to come. So by way of a change we start off this month with a few artworks:

Norfolk lavender field, Charlie and Poppy in our garden

September 2014 in our Garden

Moving swiftly on!

Monday 1st September: As it was raining all day today I decided to do some artwork in my studio first and then turn my attention to planning what needs to be done in the garden and greenhouse throughout September to get them ready for the cold, dark and wet months that lay ahead. Just because we did not get any snow or even any severe frosts last year it does not mean that this year will be the same and I must assume that we will not be as lucky this winter and plan for severe weather accordingly.

Our patio is full of flowers!

Before I make the list of jobs that will need to be done this month I took a photograph of the patio pots that are still in full bloom…

September 2014 in our Garden

The list!

As I sat at our dinning room table I wrote down the following jobs that will need to be done before winter arrives:

- Remove the black elder bush from the silver birch bed and brown bin it ready for composting.
- Remove all the plants currently in the back bed and brown bin then refresh the soil with fertilizer and fresh compost and leave unplanted over winter. I will put all of the dahlias into this bed next spring.
- Remove all dahlias from beds and pots after cutting back foliage and clean tubers, label, box and then put upstairs to over winter.
- Remove all fruit holding pots from the greenhouse then empty them of spent tomato and sweet pepper plants. Compost bin the resultant plant material before then refilling the pots with fresh compost before storing them down the outside of the greenhouse.
- Remove spent plants out of the greenhouse trough and then put small pots of plants from the patio on top of the trough to over winter.
- Re-instate the bubble wrap into the inside of the greenhouse roof and side walls to give added frost protection over the winter months.
- Place as many pots of plants as possible onto the floor of the greenhouse to over winter.
- Return the lime and lemon trees into the greenhouse to over winter.
- Re-pot into single one litre pots all of the cuttings that I took in early August and place these into the deep black plastic tray ready for putting into the sun lounge in early October to over winter.

Taking a time out for a cup of coffee and a play with the puppies I returned to my list…

September 2014 in our Garden

AND The list goes ON!

- Put pots containing lantana, olive and agapanthus inside sun lounge to over winter.
- Remove from the garden all vulnerable ornaments and put into shed to over winter.
- Bring wooden seat that is in front of the shed down to the smoke room for cleaning and then repainting with willow wood preserver. Then leave the re-treated seat to over winter in the smoke room.
- Trim the tops and sides of the hedges in the front and back gardens: **REMEMBERING NOT TO CUT IT TOO SEVERELY.**

Dahlia and a cage!

I will need to remember to empty the three cages before storing them in the shed for the winter!…

September 2014 in our Garden

The things to leave alone!

Last year I left the plants that will remain in the garden and pots over the winter un-pruned until the early spring. As this worked really well I will do the same again this year.

The Toad and his mate!

The toad and his mate will also have to be put away in the shed over the winter and I will still need to mow the grass, feed the birds, keep an eye on the plants in the greenhouse and look after our new puppies Charlie and Poppy.

Let's make a start!

As it has stopped raining there is no time like the present to get started on my list. So armed with a fork and spade I removed the black elder and disposed of it in our brown recycling bin. Being worn out by this task I spent the rest of the day on the patio with the dogs…

September 2014 in our Garden

Flying over salvias!

Tuesday 2nd September: As the plane flies over our patio bed of salvia flowers it is time for:

Setting the rules!

From day one when we got the puppies (23.08.14.) I decided that I would restrict them to the kitchen and/or the outside carport for two hours in the morning and again in the afternoon. This was so I could still do some gardening and/or artwork every day. This has worked really well so far with the dogs either sleeping or sitting at the fence watching me do whatever I have decided to do at that time. They have been really good and I always take them onto the lawn to play at the end of every session that they spend enclosed…

September 2014 in our Garden

Today is the Big Prick Day!

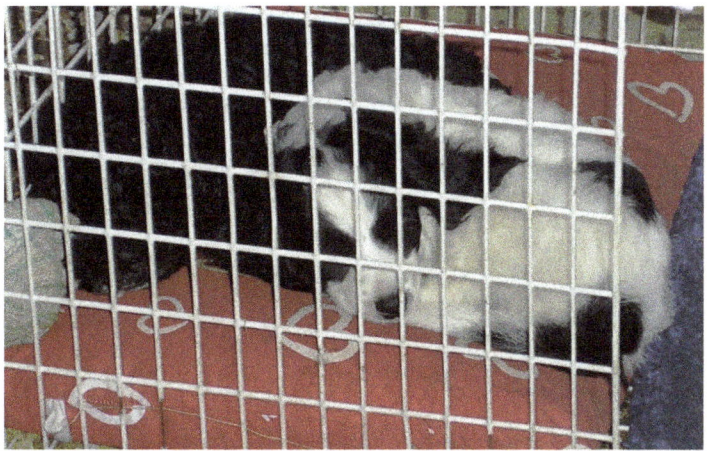

Wednesday 3rd September: Today Susie and I took the puppies to the vets for their second injection. They were very good but felt rather sorry for themselves as you can see from the photograph above.

The hoards return!

It was 10.30 am and the school children were let loose into the playground with much shouting and screaming. It is great to hear them enjoying themselves once more as they return to school after their summer holidays. After listening to the children playing for a while I decided to remove all of the plants in the back bed behind the decking and brown binned the resulting plant waste. I then planted the two Trollius "Goldkonigin" (buttercup type flowers) that we had bought at the weekend into one pot and left it on the patio to over winter before I plant it into the silver birch bed next spring. They should make a nice show next summer…

September 2014 in our Garden

Puppies playtime!

Susie in our garden watching Charlie and Poppy playing whilst the children played in the school playground over the hedge at the back of our garden…

September 2014 in our Garden

Blooming lovely!

We have had cut flowers from our garden and greenhouse trough all summer long too brighten up our lounge, dinning room and kitchen. It is great to be able to bring our garden colour into the house to enjoy.

Little house in the carport!

Thursday 4th September: Today we received the dog kennel that Susie had ordered from the Internet. Once assembled, we located it in our carport (dog area) so that when the puppies grow up they will be snug as a bug in a rug in their new home. Picture of Poppy from June 2019!...

September 2014 in our Garden

Flying over the neon!

The ruby neon salvias in our patio bed are full of flowers and they give a lovely glow of colour as the plane soars overhead.

Harvest time!

We now have a profusion of ripe tomatoes and sweet peppers so we are harvesting them daily and lovely they are too…

September 2014 in our Garden

Propagating for the future!

Seeds ready to make more new plants

Friday 5th September: Today I completed my seed sowing and cutting taking that I have planted into pots ready for putting them into the sun lounge in a large plastic tray (don't tell Susie) in early October. Like last year this should mean that we will have more than fifty free new plants to plant out next spring.

Starting the big clear up!

Saturday 6th September: Today I started the big clear up by removing the spent tomato and sweet pepper plants from their pots before storing the pots down the outside greenhouse side wall. Later that same day I pruned lightly back the buddleia as it has now finished flowering before pruning the bleeding heart down to ground level as it was also spent.

Susie to the rescue!

Sunday 7th September: Now that my right knee is much better my right foot has decided to swell up and is very painful so Susie cut the lawn for me…

September 2014 in our Garden

Putting on new growth!

Tuesday 9th September: Charlie and Poppy are growing fast and their lead training is going well. They can go out into the big wide world from this Thursday onwards…

September 2014 in our Garden

All set fair!

The weather for the last week has been warm and sunny and this is predicted to continue for the next week or so. Today was sunny and very warm reaching 25°C at 5 pm.

Getting some pills!

Wednesday 10th September: As my right foot was still very painful I went in to see my doctor first thing this morning and he gave me some pills that should do the trick!

A smaller window of opportunity!

Everyday from now on will give us gardeners a smaller and smaller window of daylight in which to garden. The sun rises later and sets earlier every day from now on. Now was the time to charge up my electric hedge trimmer battery and cut the front hedge. I plan to cut the back hedge at the weekend.

The great escape!

Thursday 11th September: We had reached the day for the dogs to venture out into the great wide world so not so much the great escape but a nice controlled walk around the village on their leads for our puppies. They loved it and were quite good and worn out from their adventure so they slept on the settee in the evening whilst Susie and I watch the TV until it was bed time.

Cutting the thatch!

Well not the sort used to thatch a cottage roof but my hair. Before taking the dogs on their evening walk I drove into Downham Market and got my hair cut…

September 2014 in our Garden

Wandering the streets!

Susie takes Charlie and Poppy out on their leads around the village every evening now. I go with them if my knees and/or right foot permits.

Dad's army!

Well not really but as I mentioned Susie is "ready each evening" with the dog leads in hand to bravely venture out with our dogs. We hope to take them to the local Forestry Commissions woods and into Downham Market at the weekend so they can meet more people, other dogs and get use to traffic and other sounds.

A weekend tale (getting ready)!

Saturday 13th and Sunday 14th September: First thing on Saturday I charged up the hedge cutter battery ready for cutting the back hedges.

Get set!

Before I rushed hedge long (sorry I mean head long) into cutting the hedge I made time for a cup of coffee. You should always find the time for a cup of coffee as any good Greek will tell you.

Go!

Having engaged my brain and armed with my set of steps, cloth to catch the off cuts, loppers for the thick stems, pruning shears for the bits near our clematis and the fully charged up hedge cutter it was time to "start the cutting"! Susie helped me by cutting the hedge back behind our central heating oil tank and I did the top and sides of the rest of the hedges before putting the off cuts into our brown bin. Then we had a rest on the decking before…

September 2014 in our Garden

Killing the weed!

After a suitable rest and recuperation period I used weed killer on the front drive as it was a fine dry day. We then took the dogs who had been very good whilst we did these task for a nice long walk in the woods.

Susie…    Alan…

You can see from the picture above just how much the hedge needed to be tamed as it had grown an awful lot this summer.

An Old Mans complaint!

When I went to see Doctor Phillip Koopowitz last Wednesday he said "I was having so much pain in my right foot because I had contracted gout". I had always thought that this was an old mans complaint but he told me that gout is a type of arthritis, typically caused by a build up of uric acid in the blood. So here I am with a left knee full of arthritis, a damaged medial ligament in my right knee and now my right foot is full of gout. **HELP!**…

September 2014 in our Garden

Putting the gout right!

The doctor gave me some pills to take which I should stop taking immediately the foot is back to normal and I have no pain. Hopefully I will soon be back to just having walking difficulties and pain in my right and left knees **ONLY!**

The sun shines on!

On a much brighter note the sun has shined on and on with the temperatures reaching 25°C most days so as the last job of the weekend I cut the back lawn.

Stop press – The expert is proved right!

Monday 15th September: Doctor Phillip Koopowitz has been proven right for this morning my right foot was back to normal and I had no pain at all in it. Hurray said I and I hope it stays that way!

It is a sign of the times!

It makes me smile that so often it is the little things that indicate change. For us every time we go into any of our clothes pockets we find little black plastic bags in them!

These are to remove any presents left by Charlie and/or Poppy on our lawn, garden or on their daily walks around the village. So the little black bags herald the new "We have Dogs" era for us…

September 2014 in our Garden

Cutting the awkward bits!

Tuesday 16th September: Taking the long loppers out of the shed I finished cutting the awkward long bits of hedge off the top at the front and back hedge that I missed at the weekend. Afterwards I completed the clear out of the greenhouse ready for us to put up the bubble wrap in the next few weeks. When we have done this I will select the plants in pots that I want to over winter and put these into the greenhouse.

A Mexican in hiding!

While looking around the patio pots to choice which ones I want to put into the greenhouse at the weekend I spied a Mexican hiding behind the lantana…

September 2014 in our Garden

Tidying up our Shed!

Wednesday 17th September: Today I finished tidying up my shed ready to put the garden ornaments into in early October to over winter.

Playtime!

Every day this week I have left the puppies to play on the lawn whilst I did my gardening jobs and apart from the odd bit of synchronised dead heading and pruning they have been very good.

Scotland decides!

Thursday 18th September: Today the people of Scotland voted as to whether they remain in the UK or go their separate way. I hope that they make the right decision and stay with us as part of Great Britain.

They voted: YES to staying in the UK – **GREAT** being the operative word – **good for them and us I think!**

Our greenhouse!

Whilst in our garden I take a last look at the greenhouse in it summer livery before starting to change its appearance, once more, ready for the coming winter…

September 2014 in our Garden

The winged visitor!

Friday 19th September: We have a pigeon who has taken to using our open ended smoke room as part of his flight path between the front and back garden. This at first caused Charlie and Poppy some concern but with my reassurance they have now taken this intrusion into their stride and they now sleep on whilst the winged visitor passes through.

Every cloud!

This week it has been dry, sunny, part cloudy and warm with temperatures at about 20°C each day. It got so hot yesterday and again today that every cloud that passed over the sun gave the dogs some welcome shade.

We even had to go down and sit in the smoke room at lunch time because the sun was too strong for Charlie and Poppy to cope with.

Bench painting!

Saturday 20th September: Having moved the bench down from the shed on Wednesday and cleaned it today. I decided to re-treat it with willow wood preserver as planned. It came up really well.

Making the bed!

Sunday 21st September: Not the sort of bed that you sleep on but our rose bed in the back garden. Susie and I removed all of the unwanted plants, raked it over and fertilised it with fish, blood and bone to help the roses next year to prosper. At the same time I trimmed back the lavender hedge at the back of this bed to encourage new strong growth next spring…

September 2014 in our Garden

Oliver Calls!

Oliver (our pheasant) still continues to come for his daily breakfast and afternoon brunch although we have had to put up some fencing across the carport exit to stop the dogs worrying him.

Home improvements!

Not for us you understand but for Charlie and Poppy. This afternoon (Sunday) we removed the old cat beds in the carport and replaced them with two new dog's beds.

The slippery slope!

Monday 22nd – Friday 26th September: All this week it has been warm and quite sunny during the day but the nights are pulling in quickly and are getting colder at below 10°C. This week I cleaned the outside glass of the greenhouse ready for Susie and I to do the inside glass and put the bubble wrap up this weekend…

Keeping watch:

I will have to keep a sharp watch on the temperatures and move my new cuttings into the sun lounge if it gets much cooler by night.

Off to Africa:
Not us you understand but the last of the swallows have disappeared from our skies this week and left the UK to return to Africa for the winter and we will very much look forward to their return in early spring.

Putting the garden to bed:
Saturday 27th September: After going early to Tesco's to do our weekly shop it was out into the garden to start putting it to bed for the winter.

Up with the bubble:
The first job was to put the bubble wrap up in the greenhouse after cleaning all the inside panes of glass.

Protecting the roses:

Next Susie and I enclosed the rose bed with 65 cm high green fencing to keep the dogs out…

Sun bathing time:

After we had completed the greenhouse and rose bed it was time to adjourn to the decking to have drinks, snacks and listen to the radio Norfolk "Garden Party" and then Norwich City FC match on the radio.

Dreaming of holiday times:

All this sunbathing reminded me of our holiday to Troulos Bay Hotel so I have included a picture of our holiday. Oh happy days. Having dreamed for a short while it was back to the radio for gardening tips and to see how Norwich got on away to Blackpool.

Top of the league (still):

Today Norwich City FC beat Blackpool FC away by 3 – 1 to go back to the top of the Championship so all was well with the world…

Taking up the dahlias:

Sunday 28th September: Today I planted three of the potted perennials that have flowered so well this summer into the silver birch bed and then commenced the removal of the dahlias and put them in the greenhouse to dry off . I removed all of the dahlias in the garden beds and pots.

Putting the ornaments to bed:

In the afternoon I removed all of the garden ornaments from their display positions and put them in the shed to over winter safely.

Moving into the sun lounge:

Monday 29th September: after waiting for Susie to go off to work I put the large plastic tray that is full of my cuttings (32 pots) into the sun lounge to over winter (perhaps Susie will not notice!). This done I decided to paint a picture:

My painting of visitors walking towards Westminster Abbey…

Brushing for victory:

Tuesday 30th September: Today armed with a stiff brush I went into the greenhouse to clean as much of the dry soil off the dahlia tubers as I could then I labelled, boxed and put them on top of the wardrobe in one of our bedrooms to over winter (Susie may not notice).

Putting the patio to bed:

Although the patio has been awash with colour this summer it was now time to empty some of the pots and prune back the geraniums, begonias, fuchsias, cape daisy, cosmos and osteospermum plants before putting them, in their pots, into the greenhouse to over winter.

The final fling:

The final job of the day was to sweep the patio up before sitting down for a celebratory Cuba Libra cocktail to toast a hard day's work…

October 2014

Around the garden in October:

Poppy looking out at the world and the re-treated bench…

Around the garden in October:

From top left to bottom right: patio baskets, patio pots, dahlias in Susie's bed near the shed and thalia and lime tree by the greenhouse...

Christmas shopping:

Wednesday 1st October: Today I decided to have a rest from the garden and puppies and go Christmas shopping in Kings Lynn. I managed to get all of the things that I wanted to get Susie for Xmas plus wrapping paper, tags, card and ribbon. I bought her… I won't tell you now just in case Susie reads my notebook before Christmas. Like her you will have to wait to see what she got! I also know what I want to get Mandy and my sisters Phyllis and Doreen for Christmas but the shop was out of stock so I will have to try again later.

The sun shines on:

When I got home I had time to spend with the puppies in the garden and have a coffee on the decking as the sun was out and it was warm.

We sat on the decking until Susie came home from work and she joined us for a glass of wine…

Wrapping up (inside):

Thursday 2nd October: This morning, as is my want, I wrapped up all of the presents that I had bought for Susie yesterday and put them upstairs on top of my wardrobe until Christmas eve.

Wrapping up (outside):

As it was still warm and sunny I completed the plan for putting the garden to bed that I had made on the 1st September. This was except putting the lime and lemon trees into the greenhouse as these pots are very heavy and I will get Susie to help me later. When Susie returned home from work she helped me to put both of the fruit tree pots into the greenhouse thus completing my putting the garden to bed for the winter plan.

As Susie and I struggled to put the last two pots into the greenhouse Charlie and Poppy watched us from the comfort of their chair on the decking...

Last few days of warm and fine weather:

The experts tell us that the weather will get much cooler and wetter after the weekend and the temperatures that have been about 20°C will plummet. So while we wait for this to happen lets cheer ourselves up with some October colour:

The fuchsia "Mothers pride" and the Lofos climbing plants are still in full bloom in our garden…

Welcome to the twilight zone:

Saturday 4th October: As the nights pull in and we get less and less daylight we are now entering the "twilight zone" of autumn. Let us have a look at some of my preparation for the winter in our garden:

Top: Alan after fencing the rose bed ready for next spring – Bottom: The patio pots emptied of plants…

Charlie and Poppy update:

Sunday 5th October: We have now had the puppies for five weeks now and they are growing fast, settling in well and sleeping through the night since day one. Oh happy us!

Charlie   Poppy

More cuttings:

Susie helped me put the last tray of plant cuttings that I took some weeks ago into the greenhouse to over winter…

Plants all in:

The greenhouse is now protected by bubble wrap and we have filled it full of potted plants to over winter:

The picture above was taken just prior to Susie and I putting the fruit trees in so as you can see there is not much room left in the greenhouse.

The finishing touches:

Monday 6th October – Friday 10th October: Now that we have completed putting the back garden to bed for the winter we just had the front sage hedge to cut and a few pots to empty. I did this during the week and on Friday I took eight large full bags of waste plant material down to the local recycling centre for them to compost...

Mary came bearing gifts:

Saturday 11th October: Mary who lives in a bungalow across the road from our house has for the last few years brought us apples and pears off her fruit trees at this time of the year. We are always pleased to see her and appreciate her kindness greatly especially me as Susie then makes delicious apple pies and pear desserts from them that we enjoy with our evening meals all week. When she called today she passed comment on how nice the salvias "hot lips", "Ruby Neon" and "Royal Red" plants looked so I offered to raise her some cutting of each next spring so she to can have these beautiful plants in her garden next year.

Above is the patio bed with ruby neon salvias (now cut back) that have flowered all spring, summer and into late autumn…

Winter arrives:

Sunday 12th October: Today we woke up to white grass and a temperature of only 4°C so this signals the start of winter.

The useful fairy:

Not the sort with wings and a wand you understand but the sort that comes in a squeeze plastic bottle that you use to do your dirty dishes. When Susie was still at school up in Derbyshire she use to work weekends at a café in Hathersage where the owner instructed the waitresses to use neat fairy liquid on a clean cloth to wipe the insides of the cafes windows. This was because it prevented condensation from forming and kept the windows clear so customers could see out and more importantly prospective customers could see in. Susie told me this story last year and I asked her to do the same to the inside greenhouse glass last autumn to keep the windows clear and she repeated the treatment again today.

It really works so give it a try.

The good fairy…

Last chance maybe:

Although the day started quite cold it had stayed dry and slowly the temperature had managed to creep up to 17°C by 4 pm. So Susie had taken the opportunity to dry our weekly wash on the outside clothes rotary line (possibly for the last time this year) and I cut the lawn (probably not for the last time this year)! After playing with the puppies with some of their toy's we all managed to sit on the decking and listen to the BBC 4 Gardeners Question Time programme at 2 pm and have a drink…

Raising the wire:

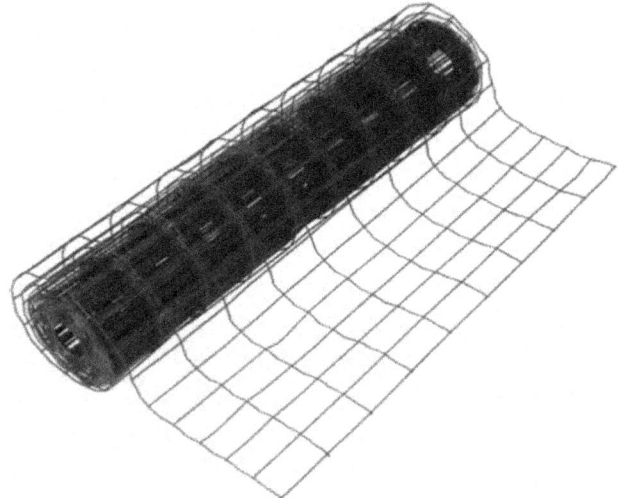

Monday 13th – Thursday 16th October: The weather continues to be cold (below 10°C) and wet but between showers I have still managed to do some extra jobs outside. After pruning the salvias back to just above the soil surface we found that Poppy could now jump onto the patio wall and then down into the patio. We wanted to avoid the risk of her injuring herself as well as discourage her from going onto the patio alone so how could we achieve this. Luckily my wonderful shed came to the rescue once more. How you might ask? Well my shed is full of stored wonderful things and amongst these treasures was a length of green chicken wire which turned out to be the exact length that we required to raise the height of our patio defences. We hammered bamboo stakes (also from the shed) at intervals along the patio bed next to the wall and then secured the chicken wire to the stakes. This raised the defences by 60 cm thus stopping Poppy being able to jump on the wall and then down into the patio. Mission accomplished.

An added bonus:

By putting the chicken wire in place we decided that this will in fact be an added bonus by stopping the salvias from being able to cascade over the patio wall whilst giving them helpful support next spring and summer. Who said "good will come from bad" I do not know but for us that statement has proven correct once again…

It's raining again!:

Friday 17th October: Today it rained all day but once again good comes from bad as the dogs laid asleep in the their basket in the kitchen I prepared a sheet of watercolour paper onto my painting board, got out my paint box and brushes to paint at the dinning room table (my art studio) for the day.

My painting is entitled "Girl Talk" in which I have, using my memory of my long ago school days, I tried to capture some girls standing outside the school gates chatting as they so often did back then…

Swapping one paint brush for a roller:

Saturday 18th – Sunday 19th October: Over the weekend Susie and I retrieved the tins of paint, trays, floor coverings and rollers from our loft in preparation for re-commencing our indoor house re-decorating programme that we started last year. We will, over the next few weeks re-decorate the following rooms:
1. The dinning room
2. The kitchen
3. Ginny's room
4. Guest room

Once these are done we will have completely re-decorated all fourteen rooms in our home in the last twelve months.

Not forgetting the garden:

Rather than just sitting relaxing in our garden, weather permitting, it will still require ongoing attention throughout October and for the rest of the winter months. I will still need to feed the birds and give them fresh water daily, keep an eye on the plants in the greenhouse and the dreaded lawn may need a trim from time to time…

Oliver leaves home:

Monday 20th – Friday 24th October: This week has been very eventful first with the dogs spending more and more time running around the garden Oliver, our pheasant, has decided that it is all to boisterous for him and has therefore, moved to new winter quarters elsewhere. We wish him well and if he should return we will welcome him back happily.

The dog's (Poppy and Charlie) playing on the lawn in October

Putting the shorts to bed:

I have been wearing shorts for the last six months but like all good things, due to the weather getting colder, this has come to an end. So it is long trousers for me and this reminds me of when I was at school many, many years ago. My mother would make we wear long trousers when we returned to school after the summer holidays and not allow me to go back into shorts until the following Easter. It just shows you that retiring to our garden has allowed me to time travel back in time and wear shorts all spring and summer just as I did in my school days…

Kestrel calling:

This week has also seen the arrival of a Kestrel which was flying and circling above our garden. In the last few days it has taken to swooping down trying to capture his prey (our poor birds) in our garden. Thankfully he has missed his target so far which I am pleased about but it is only a matter of time before he makes a kill. It is great to see one of natures wild birds of prey in action and at such close quarters and I hope that he keeps trying and failing so I can see him again and again.

Jar, Jar Binks:

Animals do the funniest of things and our puppy Poppy is no exception. She has started to hunt but in a very funny way. Every evening when we are sitting in our outside smoke room with the lights on (from 5 pm because it is getting dark early now) we sit and watch her jumping as high as she can to try and catch some very small insects attracted by the light. This in itself is quite funny but what is even funnier is that every time she jumps her long floppy ears turn inside out and she looks just like Jar, Jar Binks a character out of Star Wars!

We laugh and call her Jar, Jar but her brother Charlie just lays there and look's at her as if to say "whatever" silly girl…

The early Christmas present:

During this week I also posted my first early Christmas present to Thordis Fredrickson the host of BBC Radio Norfolk programme called "The Garden Party". I sent her a signed copy of my first book called "Retiring to the garden – Year 1" as a gift to say thank you to her and her panel for all the help and advice they give us gardeners in Norfolk. We ourselves have sort advice from them in the past (see page 95 of my first book) and acted upon it to good effect so I thought a small token of our appreciation would not go amiss.

Turning back time:

Saturday 25th October: Tonight we in the UK welcome winter in by turning the clocks back one hour so it will be getting darker that bit earlier from now on!

Cuttings for Mary:

On Saturday morning as the weather was bright and the temperature was about 14°C I decided to pot up 12 salvia cuttings for our neighbour Mary now rather than waiting until next spring.

I still had a small amount of floor space available in the greenhouse and I thought I may as well use this up with the salvia cuttings and over winter these so I can give them to Mary earlier than originally planned next spring hopefully…

News flash: Plant savaged by pack of dogs:

Sunday 26th October: Today our puppies attacked and removed a long branch off of our Akebia Quinata growing up our silver birch tree. This is an evergreen climber that has clusters of chocolate scented blooms from March to May. We have been nurturing this plant for 3 years and it has climbed to more than 3 metres up the tree in that time. So as you can imagine we were very unhappy with the puppies for their unauthorised pruning exploits!

We needed to protect it from further damage so finding some unused fencing in my shed I set about protecting it from the beasts maybe, in hindsight I should have done this before the dogs arrived. Not wishing to finish this episode negatively I used the branch that the dogs had ripped off the plant to take two cuttings from and potted these up in the hope that they rooted and we would end up with two new plants.

Unleashing the beasts:

Well not the beasts exactly but Poppy and Charlie who Susie now unleashes when they go for a walk in the local forestry commission woods. This was a significant step for our now four month old puppies and they responded by returning to Susie whenever she called them so we were well pleased. When we got home from the woods we put the dogs to bed and set off to the Range in Kings Lynn to buy four rolls of 10 metre x 1 metre high fencing and 30 wooden posts so we could further restrict our dogs from going into most of my precious flower beds...

Pictures in the garden in late October:

The weather in October has been unusually mild and even at the end of the month Susie was still able to dry our weekly wash on the line outside. When we got home from our trip to get some fencing and posts we were able to go down and sit on the decking with the puppies and enjoy the late autumn sunshine…

Preparing the way:

Monday 27th – Friday 31st October: This week, weather permitting, I will prepare the way for us erecting our new fencing by marking out where we want to put the new fencing using a string line, re-edge the lawn 5 cm away from where the fencing will be and then hammer in the new posts into position every 2 metres. This is because Susie is on holiday as from this Thursday until next Wednesday (5th November) and she has promised to help me erect our new fencing.

Early completion:

By Wednesday lunchtime I had completed all of the preparation and then with Susie's help we completed the erection of our new fencing by Friday afternoon. When we had finished we had excluded the puppies from all of our flowers beds leaving just three areas of soil and plants available to them plus of course the whole of the lawn. We did all this with the dogs watching on from their bed on the arbour and when we let them into the garden they seemed happy with the areas they had left to explore and use for their continued gardening exploits.

So when we finished all our work and their inspection it was time to go indoors for everyone to have a rest in the front room…

Paintings painted in the month of October:

Paintings featured: Dulux Dogs – Nut Stall in Skiathos…

November 2014

It is official (I am OLD):

This month I reach the ripe old age of 65 and so I will start to receive my state pension and this is when I guess you begin to get officially OLD. This additional income (I already receive my company pension) will boast our funds that we have available to pay the ever increasing bills that we face. To celebrate my birthday and becoming an O.A.P. (old aged pensioner) I painted the following watercolour:

The above painting is of Big Ben in London that looks down on the Houses of Parliament whose members have so kindly deemed me old enough to receive my state pension from the public purse. **Thank you…**

Sunbathing in November in the UK:

Saturday 1st November: Today was blue sky and warm sunshine with temperatures reaching 19°C. Yes it was that hot in the UK in November so we spent the day sunbathing on the decking with the puppies admiring our new fencing although I do not think the dogs were that impressed! Ginny and Bertie her dog came to see us and the dogs all played well together after Charlie and Poppy got used to how tall Bertie was.

Poppy exploring the newly fenced off garden…

After the Lord Mayor's precession:

Sunday 2nd November: Today was the complete opposite to yesterday and was cold with heavy rain all day. This was typical of the UK with glorious sunshine yesterday followed by heavy rain today it reminded me of what people say follows the Lord Mayors precession (first the splendour of the occasion and then it is back to the everyday drabness). So being stuck indoors I went into my art studio (the dinning room table) and painted the following watercolour painting:

My painting is of the harbour wall at Mousehole in Cornwall where we holidayed in November 2012. Our apartment was called the Sandpiper and is on the upper floor of the white building featured…

The return of Franky:

Franky painted in March 2015

Monday 3rd November: Today the weather was much improved and best of all our friends Andrew and Lynn with their dog Franky came for lunch:

Franky and his family (Andrew and Lynn with Poppy and Charlie) pictured on their last visit to us in August this year…

Blowing down the vane:

Tuesday 4th November: The weather vane that is on our shed and that was blown down and damaged last year has once again been blown down by the strong winds that greeted us this morning. It is sad but I picked up the pieces and put them in the shed and we will re-think if we bother to get it repaired again or replace it with a new stronger one!

The shed minus the weather vane!

Puppies first Fireworks Night:

Wednesday 5th November: Traditionally in the UK today people celebrate the attempt to blow up the Houses of Parliament by Guy Fawkes (many years ago which failed) by letting off fire works. In recent years the traditional day has been largely ignored and now people let off fireworks for several days before and after the 5th and so we were concerned just how this would affect our young puppies. We need not have worried as they took it in their stride and just continued to sleep, play or do whatever they were doing at the time…

Inside-out:

Thursday 6th – Sunday 9th November: The weather in November continued to be mixed with some days cold and wet and others being warmer (10°C) with some blue sky and sunshine so it was a matter of being out when you could or inside if you must! Below are some photographs that were taken outside during this period:

The Puppies – Susie watering the greenhouse and the last cut flowers - The back of our house…

News flash: Decorating to be delayed:

We have decided to delay our planned indoor decorating until next spring because my knees are still very painful and the dogs need more time to settle before we get out the decorating equipment. I must say I am quite relieved and to make me even happier I painted a painting of our holiday hotel to make my smile even wider:

The Troulos Bay Hotel on Skiathos

Hey presto:

Monday 10th – Sunday 30th November: Our daughter Ginny gave me a set of three branch style solar lights for my birthday. These have a profusion of small lights on each branch and hey presto once it was charged up the lights came on and looked lovely in our silver birch bed. Unfortunately they do not stay on very long because of the lack of sunshine at this time of the year but will look great next spring and summer as the days get longer and the sun gets stronger…

Leaf mould:

During the month of November I always collect the fallen leaves off of the trees and bag them up into empty compost bags and store over winter ready to mix with new compost next spring. I then use this mix to top dress our flower beds to enrich the soil and boast the plants.

Back garden patio in late November and the new fencing to keep the dogs off the flower beds.

The last cut:

On the 19th November I cut the back lawn for the last time this year and cleaned my mower before putting it away in the shed to over winter. I also finished reading the new Lee Child book called "Personal" that Susie gave me for my birthday and enjoyed Reacher's latest adventure very much…

A time for rest:

Now that we are in the ever increasing grip of the winter months when temperatures are plummeting (at least -3°C most nights) there is very little work that can be done in the garden so for the next few months it will be just a case of keeping the birds fed and watered and looking after the new plant cuttings in the greenhouse and sun lounge. These are the months when I spend most of my time indoors writing, reading or producing watercolour paintings.

My painting called: Sailing off Skiathos…

Another one bites the dust:

It seemed only a few days ago that we entered November and now it is time to leave this behind and head into the seasonal month of good cheer that is December. On the last day of November I produced the following artwork to cheer me up and to help me remember a good friend called George of the Mythos Café, The Old Port in Skiathos Town.

Boats in Skiathos Bay Harbour…

A winter warmer:

It is always great to sit by our open log fire in the lounge on a cold winter's night when the temperatures are below 0°C and think of friends and warmer days spent in the garden or on holiday. As I sit by the fire very quietly I can almost hear the sound of jingle bells as Santa gets ready for his big day next month…

December 2014

The holly and the ivy:

During our dog walks in the local wood this month we have had the opportunity to gather some holly and ivy which Susie has used to help decorate the house ready for putting our Christmas tree up and celebrating our first Xmas with Poppy and Charlie.

Sing for your supper:

Although I spend much of my time at the moment in my studio! I still have to daily go into the garden to do small jobs and one big task. Every day throughout the winter months, twice a day one of us will need to keep the eight bird feeding containers and the bowl of fresh drinking water filled. We provide for our feathered friends nuts, fat balls and mixed seed. We have regular visits from woodpeckers, blue tits, coal tits, long tailed tits, great tits, sparrows, collared doves, siskins, goldfinches, wood pigeons, jay, wren and even the very seasonal robin.

Artwork of The Fine City of Norwich…

More of my watercolour paintings painted in December:

Debbie Harry (Blondie)

Boats in Mousehole Harbour Cornwall…

Thanking a hero:

Saturday 13th December: Susie and I drove to the Red Lion PH in Eaton, Norwich to meet my sister Phyllis and her husband Dennis along with my sister Doreen and her partner Tony for lunch. This gave me the opportunity to say a BIG thank you to Dennis who is one of my gardening hero's. Many years ago I would go and stay with them and it was his example of great gardening that I realised in later life had inspired me to plan and plant my garden so it was full of beautiful flowers and fruits. I think he was both surprised and pleased to get this long overdue recognition for the important example he gave me in how to garden well and with pride.

Phyllis and Dennis - Alan and Doreen at the Red Lion

A snip for Christmas:

Monday 22nd December: Today our 6 month old male puppy went to the vets to have the snip! This operation will mean that he cannot become a Dad in the future…

A Merry Christmas to all my readers!

To finish December on a festive note I give you the following artwork just for **YOU...**

Santa Claws!

Festive thoughts:

I wonder what delights Susie will get me this year. She has a habit of buying me things for the garden, books to read, painting equipment to use and sweeties. I just can not wait to see what presents Santa brings me this year.

A Christmas Wish:

Have a safe and Happy Christmas and a successful gardening New Year.

See you all again next year...

January 2015

Day ONE of a new year and I wish:

We always start a new year with optimism. This year is no different. I wish for peace and good health to all and for myself I want to be able to grow most of the plants I use in our garden again this year from seeds and cuttings that I have personally propagated. Other things we are resolved to do this year are:

- Buy new enamel flower plaques for either side of our front door
- Make further improvements to our dog defences
- Construct a new high level flower display shelf on our fence facing our carport seating area

My first watercolour painting of a new year:

Down the Pit: Painted on the 1st January 2015 as a tribute to the brave coal miners waiting to go down the lift shaft to the coal face…

Illumination:

Thursday 1st January 2015: We started the New Year much as we did last New Years day by donning our winter coats and gloves to spend the day out in the garden. Unlike last year we did not have any fences to mend as the wire binding that we used last year to secure our fence panels in place has worked a treat and the panels have stayed in place securely. This New Years day we have decided to put an additional outside light on our back kitchen wall so it will illuminate the patio and lawn so us and the dogs can venture out in the darkness and see where we are going! We went to B&Q and got an outside light fitting, bulb, plug, wire clips and five metres of three core heavy duty black wire then it was home to install our new lighting system. We have decided to bring the wire from a kitchen socket through the wall and fix the wire along the wall and into the light fitting. We started at 11 am by fixing the fitting to the outside wall and then wired it up before fixing the wire to the wall and into the kitchen through the pre-drilled hole and after putting the plug on we put it into the wall socket. After putting a bulb into the light fitting it was time to see if our new lighting worked? The answer was YES and we were well pleased with our efforts and enjoyed an illuminated patio and lawn that same evening. Well back to the studio.

Artwork above: The Tears of the Clown…

In the deep mid-winter:

Friday January 2nd – Friday 9th January: As we progress into January I am please to say that apart from some strong winds and frosts over night we have not as yet had any snow unlike Susie's Mum who lives in Sheffield as they have had significant snow falls already this winter. Apart from feeding the birds daily I have spent most of my time this week indoors reading, writing and watercolour painting in my studio.

Out and about in London: Two paintings the same but different…

Dabbling on:

Saturday 10th January – Thursday 27th January: The weather has continued to be cold and means that I have had to spend much of my time indoors over the last few weeks however, this has also given me plenty of opportunity to dabble in my favourite hobby of watercolour painting. Below are examples of some of the painting I have completed this month:

All tied up in Skiathos Town harbour

Mousehole harbour in Cornwall…

The awakening:

Saturday 31st January: Today there was a light dusting of snow which lasted only a few minutes but did not settle however, more is expected tomorrow so we may still have some snow this year for the puppies to wonder at. Today the garden had the first signs of a coming spring with the snowdrops in flower and the other spring bulbs also beginning to send up new growth in the garden:

I was even able to do a bit of gardening yesterday as it was bright and sunny although quite cold. I tidied up the pots on the patio, checked progress in the greenhouse before feeding the birds then it was back indoors for coffee. Today I also received an appointment for Friday 13th February 10.40 am: with Mr. Jeffery's my orthopaedic surgeon at the Queen Elizabeth Hospital, Kings Lynn to see what can be done for my poorly knees…

Success while waiting for better weather:

Wednesday 28th January – Saturday 31st January: Another month has passed and still no sign of the white stuff (snow) but it continues to be cold, wet and windy most days so I am spending my days indoors writing and painting. In the last few days I have completed my latest book and submitted it to the publishers for proof reading and then printing so very soon I will be the proud author of two books.

Once published my latest book will be available on Amazon and other good Internet providers in E-Book and Paperback format. My book this time will showcase my art along with the story of the memories that inspired them…

In anticipation:

In anticipation of my pending new book publication I sat in my studio and produced some more watercolour paintings:

Sebastian the Tiger and Sailing Away

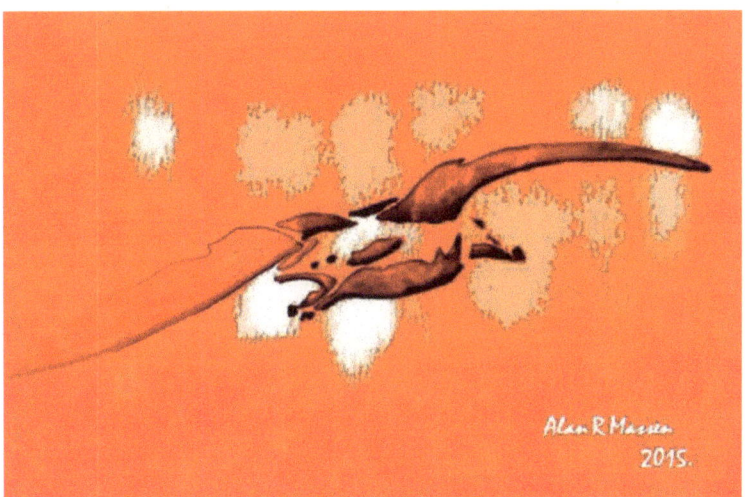

The Lone Albatross…

February 2015

Planning for spring:

Sunday 1st February – Thursday 12th February: Now that we are into February we can start to plan for the new gardening season. As is usually the case we have received several plant and seed catalogues from suppliers and although we do not plan to buy any new plants from these sources I have used these to identify what new perennial plants I would like for our garden. These are:

- Rudbeckia "Summerina"
- Dwarf Mallow "Barnsley Baby"
- Calendula "Winter Wonders"
- Dwarf Verbena "Lollipop"
- Geranium "Rozanne"
- Alstromeria "Indian Summer"
- Penstemon " Ice Cream"
- Chrysanthemum "Decorative"
- Chrysanthemum "Incurved"
- Gerbera "Sweet Collection"
- Sun Diascia "Eternal Flames"
- Salvia "Autumn Moon"
- Echinacea "Flamingo"
- Echinacea "Cantaloupe"
- Penstemon "Electric Blue"

I have put a copy of this list into my wallet so when we go to either the Moat or other local garden centre's we can look out for them as we stock up with trays of annuals to brighten up our summer beds, baskets and pots…

In the deep mid-winter:

Monday 2nd February - Thursday 12th February: We are now in the firm grip of winter with cold winds from the north and/or east and snow, sleet and/or rain every day. Because of this I sat in my studio and produced some more watercolour paintings:

Newquay Harbour Cornwall

Polperro Harbour Cornwall…

Mack the knife:

Friday 13th February – 10.40 am: Today I have an appointment with... Well not "Mack the knife" exactly but Mr. Jeffery's my orthopaedic surgeon at the Queen Elizabeth Hospital, Kings Lynn. My GP Doctor Phillip Koopowitz referred me to the surgeon after my last visit to see him because I was finding it increasingly difficult to manage the pain and immobility of my left knee and at the same time my right knee's damaged medial ligament was still causing me problems after eight months. My Doctor now felt it was time to go under the knife and have my worn out left knee joint removed and replaced with a shinny new metal artificial knee.

Off to see the wizard:

So on the appointed day Susie, who had taken the day off work to accompany me, and I set off. I felt very nervous and hoped that Mr Jeffery's was indeed the wizard that would wave his magic scrapple and take away all the years of pain that my left knee had caused me. I also hoped that he would be able to suggest ways in which to improve the swift recovery of my right knee as I would need this to be fully operational and pain free should I have a full knee replacement operation!

Monty Cat and Rex the Dog…

Going under the knife! - The man from the hospital (Mr. Jeffery's) he says: YES…

Susie and I arrived at the hospital just after 9 am went in and after having an x-ray we went in to see the specialist at 11.50 am. After examining my knees and referring to the x-ray he said that my left knee was worn out and in need of urgent replacing.

He will perform a total knee replacement and that he would do the operation in the next two to three months. He also said that he will revisit my right knee if it is still a problem after I recover fully from the surgery which will take about three to six months after I undergo the left knee replacement operation.

After returning home I decided to paint a watercolour to cheer me up:

The Sleepy Cat and The flower stall on Norwich market…

Valentines Day:

Saturday 14th February: Is traditionally the day you tell the one you love that they are very special and give them a token of your love. To this end I gave Susie a card and some silver earrings that she liked and a few other bits and pieces. Susie gave me some gardening tools and a garden stool which I was very pleased with and will use when out deadheading this year in the garden.

The start of a new gardening season:

Today is also the first day of the new gardening season when I always prune back my early spring flowering clematis. So gifts given and pruning done I returned to my studio to do some artwork while I wait for improved weather conditions so I can get the gardening underway for another exciting year.

Artwork of Polly and Orang-utan…

The Norfolk Boy:

Roy came round and told me that my new book **"Retiring into a Rainbow"** has been sent to the printers for publishing and I will receive my first copies of my new book next Wednesday 18th February. This is very exciting news indeed. He also told me that our house is very cold for him as I do not have the heating on during the day and he thought this was down to us Norfolk boys not feeling the cold. I told him it is more down to me spending much of my time in our garden with the dogs. To celebrate the imminent arrive of my new book I painted another painting:

Wells…

The above artwork is called: "My Bleeding Heart". Why this title: this will become apparent when you turn to the next page…

SAD News:

We have had to cancel our planned holiday to our paradise Greek Island of Skiathos for later this year because of my forthcoming knee operation. We will miss seeing everyone at the Troulos Bay Hotel, Mythos Café Skiathos Old Port and our good friends Alistair, Issy, Karl, Anna, Andrew and Lynn very much but if everything goes well with my surgery we will be back to see them all again in the future.

Memories of Skiathos and the people of Troulos Bay Hotel…

More defences:

Sunday 15th February: Today Susie and I went to the Range to get two more 10 metre rolls of 1 metre high fencing to finish our dog defences of the remaining flower beds still unprotected. Susie is on holiday from work this week and so weather permitting we hope to erect the new fencing sometime this week. We arrived home at about 11.30 am and as it was blue sky, sunny and about 8°C we decided to make a start on erecting the new fencing around Susie's bed and the rose bed. We finished this at about 3 pm so we sat on the decking with the puppies and enjoyed our first sunbathing session of the New Year.

SAD NEWS: We have lost our Marble:

Monday 16th February: Not the glass sort of marbles that children use but our cat Marble. He did not come home yesterday for his tea so this morning Susie went out to search for him.

Whilst out Susie heard that a cat was run over and badly hurt yesterday so we fear the worse. I telephoned the local vet's in our area to see if anyone had brought an injured tabby cat into them but unfortunately not. On Tuesday 17th February I prepared the last two beds for fencing later on in the week and again Susie and I managed to sit in the sun on the decking for awhile and concluded that as our cat has still not returned home we must resign ourselves to his loss and hope that he did not suffer to much…

Friends comes bearing gifts:

Wednesday 18th February: Our friends Corri and Roy came for lunch today bearing gifts. They gave me the first five copies of my new book "Retiring into a Rainbow".

Alan in the February sun…

It looked fantastic and Roy will be ordering me twenty four more copies today so I can give them as gifts to friends and family. He also did some research for me on upgrading my current computer and recommended one that he had seen in PC World in Kings Lynn to me. Susie and I will go and take a look for ourselves on Friday when we go to The Range to look for wall plaques and a new dog bed for the back of Susie's car…

Finishing the job:

Thursday 19th February: Today Susie and I finished off fencing the remaining two beds in the back garden so that now all of the flower beds are protected and the puppies are fully enclosed on the lawn (what's left of it). Susie say's it looks more like a rugby pitch now rather than a lawn.

We hope that the grass will grow back in the spring where the puppies have worn it through racing each other about…

Everything is going to plan:

Friday 20th February: We went to The Range, as planned, this morning and selected a new puppy bed for the back of Susie's car and three new metal wall plaques. These we fitted outside on Saturday morning. Whilst in Kings Lynn we also went to PC World and had a look at the computer that Roy recommended and we fully agree with his assessment that the model he chose "HP Pavilion 23" would be the ideal upgrade machine for me. All I have to do now is save up for it! Two of the plaques went either side of our front door and the third a cockerel plaque I fixed to the back shed door.

Ellie waiting for the first day of spring…

The final Day:

Sunday 22nd February: Today is the last day of Susie's week long holiday from work which has been quite eventful. First we went to the hospital on the Friday followed by the loss of our cat Marble on the Sunday then it was fence erection duties Monday too Thursday and finally metal wall plaque fixing on the Saturday. So we have done quite a lot of things this week. We even had some time to sit outside in the sun on the arbour with the puppies.

Poppy and Charlie Then…

Now…

The week finished on quite a cloudy and cold note (4°C) so I hope next week when Susie goes back to work the puppies and I get some sun and blue skies…

Keeping my fingers crossed for Snowdrops without the snow:

Monday 23rd February – Saturday 28th February: We finished the month still without any severe/heavy frosts and we have only had a slight sprinkling of snow on the ground for two days so far this winter. So I am keeping my fingers crossed that this state of affairs continues for the next few weeks.

Going WILD:

Now that spring is approaching Susie and I discussed how we are going to plant up the garden this year bearing in mind that I will be going into hospital sometime soon and may be unable to help her much in the garden this year. With this in mind we will plant out our over wintered dahlias into the back bed as soon as we can and follow this up with planting all the cuttings that I have nurtured in the greenhouse and sun lounge into patio pots. In addition to this we will be seeding the silver birch bed this year with a mix of **WILD** flower seeds that Susie got from Tesco. The other back garden beds and front beds and pots will be left as they are as these are already fully planted up with perennials from last year. We will only buy a few bedding plants to give our baskets, pots and beds a splash of summer colour from the Moat nursery…

March 2015

The Mad March Hare:

Poppy in 2019...

Sunday 1st March: Today is the first day of spring and traditionally the time for mad March hares but for us the longer days of sunlight and the slight raising of temperature (9 °C) means that our puppies Charlie and Poppy can charge around the garden for longer causing mayhem and destruction. They have such fun and really do very little damage…

The plant gatherer:

Sunday 1st: Early this morning Susie and I went to do our weekly shopping at Tesco's in Kings Lynn. While Susie went around the supermarket I first went into the café and had a coffee (you should always find time for a coffee) before going into Dobbie's garden centre (attached to Tesco's) and managed to find several tubers, bulbs and plants for this year's garden:

- **Asiatic Lily (hardy) - Yellow flowers**
- **Vinca "illumination" – Blue flowers**
- **Dahlia "Bishop of York" – Yellow flowers**
- **Dahlia "Bishop of Llandaff" – Red flowers**
- **Dahlia "Painted Lady" – Pink and White flowers**
- **Zantedeschia "Auckland" – Pink flowers**
- **Canna "Angel Martin" – Yellow and Pink flowers**
- **Canna "Stuttgart" – Yellow and Orange flowers**
- **Bessera "Elegans" – Red flowers**
- **Crocosmia "Emily Mckenzie" – Orange flowers**

Susie was well pleased when she joined me after completing our weekly food shop and we returned home happy.

The crazy Canaries:

Carrow Road…

Later that same day at 2.05 pm to be exact Norwich City FC kicked off against local rivals Ipswich Town at Carrow Road. As usual I listened to the match on BBC Radio Norfolk and City won by 2 – 0. The fans and I went crazy because Norwich are now 3rd in the championship and maybe heading back to the Premiership come next May. Oh I do so hope so…

Hanging it all out!

While I was listening to the football and enjoying a glass of beer Susie was busy out in the garden hanging out the washing for the very first time this year as it was blue skies, sunny and temperature of 9 °C. So not only had my beloved City won today but our cloths were all dried out in the fresh first day air of March.

Two dozen of the best:

Monday 2nd March: Today Roy my book publisher called around and gave me 24 more copies of my latest paperback book **"Retiring into a Rainbow".** He also suggested that we produce a **"Table Top Edition"** of this book in hardback printed on thicker paper and with a very high quality print finish.

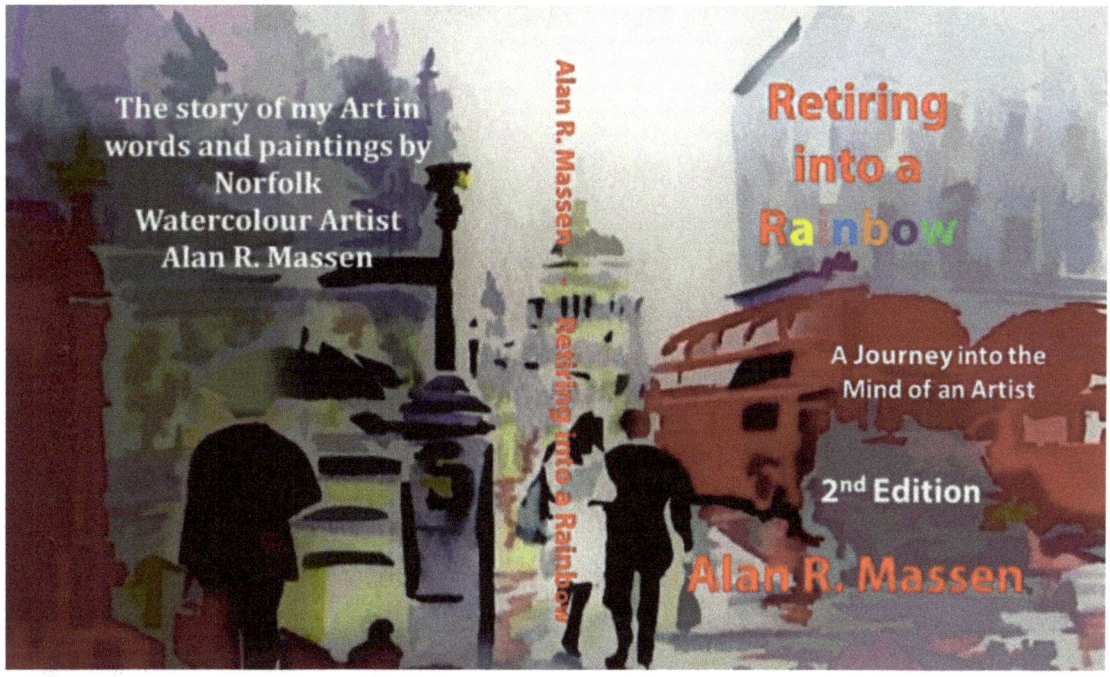

This we worked on at the dining room table before he left to continue reworking the front cover at his before sending it off to the printers for production. We will also put this and the paperback and EBook onto Amazon for distribution in the USA, Germany and Australia and of course the UK…

Tub of goodness:

Wednesday 4th March: Today we had delivered a large 10 kg tub of Blood, Fish and Bone fertiliser ready for us to use when we plant up our new plants into the beds and pots in April. Susie had ordered it online on Sunday so it was quite a quick delivery.

When Kevin's cleaning windows:

Thursday 5th March: Today at 3 pm Kevin our window cleaner arrived and said because of my poorly knees he would transfer his ladders over the barrier in our smoke room to save me having to take the barrier down. That's just the sort of good bloke he is.

He always asks how Susie and Ginny are doing and whilst we had one of our usual frank exchanges of views (we put the world to rights) I took the above pictures to go into this book. When he asked me why I told him I had become an author and showed him my latest book **"Retiring into a Rainbow"**. He liked it and I promised him a paperback copy of this book when it is published…

Good old Royal Mail:

After Kevin had left I took twelve of my parcels of my latest book down to the local Post Office and posted copies out to friends and family. They were relatively inexpensive to send and I was pleased with the quality of service that Royal Mail gave me. Well done to them.

More paintings:

Friday 6th March: Having spent most of the week re-working my latest books I decided to get the watercolour paint box, paper and brushes out and do a painting:

Painting called: Highland Cattle

When I had completed the above watercolour it was time for a rest before I begin the hard work in our garden that l plan to do this weekend…

The hard weekend:

Saturday 7th and Sunday 8th March: All this weekend I spent in our sun lounge updating all my book files on my old computer and saving the new files onto a large capacity stick. I was doing this because Susie had said that I could use her laptop on the dining room table while I wait to save enough money to buy myself a swanky new computer. She had also got me a wireless mouse and keyboard so I could sit in our dining room and have the puppies in there with me rather than shutting them away when I am in the sun lounge writing things such as this book onto my computer. This activity took me all day Saturday and up to 3 pm on Sunday but then I was able, with Susie help, to put my files onto her laptop… I am now using my new location and her laptop as you read!

More painting:

Monday 9th March: As a reward for all my efforts at the weekend I decided today to do another painting:

My painting called: Wild Horses…

More plants:

Tuesday 10th March: Today as I have been stuck inside for two weeks now I decided to risk a trip out in my car this morning. Where was I to go? Well that was obvious I would go to Downham Market Country Store and look at some more plants and bulbs. I managed to get the following:

- **Strelitzia "Reginae" patio plant**
- **Crocosmia "Mount Usher" Yellow flower bulbs**

Arriving home my knees felt like they were about to explode and the pain was intense but it was worth it to get out for a little while, give the car a run out and get a few more delights for this summer's garden display.

Hardbacks:

In the afternoon Roy arrived with three copies of my book **"Retiring into a Rainbow"** hardback books. One we will keep and the other two we will give one each to our daughters Mandy and Ginny.

On the
wings of a Dove…

In the evening my sister Phyllis and Susie's Mum Ann phoned to thank me for sending them a copy of my latest paperback book. That was nice of them and I thanked them for their kind words. I was very pleased to hear how quickly they had arrived. Well done and thank you Royal Mail…

It's painting time:

Wednesday 11th to Friday 13th March: After all the work on my books and bringing the writing up to date on this book I decided to spend the rest of the week doing a few more paintings:

Painting inspired by Kevin called: When I'm cleaning windows

Artwork: Lady in Lavender…

Getting ready:

Saturday 14th and Sunday 15th: This weekend Susie and I, well actually more Susie than me, cleared and pruned back last year's plants in the beds ready for them to put on more new growth this spring. On Sunday Ginny came round with her dog Bertie and along with Susie, Charlie and Poppy they all went down to the local warren for a walk. I stayed at home with my poorly knees.

Mothers Day:

Afterwards Ginny cooked us all a meal as a thank you present for her mum this **"Mothers Days"**…

It is dangerous out there!

Monday 16th March – Friday 20th March: We had some very sad news at the weekend Susie Brother Pete had been rushed into hospital where he died on Sunday morning so Susie had Monday off work as she tried to come to terms with losing her brother. As it was a nice day I suggested that we do some work in the garden as this may help Susie to be outside doing something. As always she worked hard and finished pruning back last year's perennials and weeding all of the flower beds. Whilst doing this she managed to poke herself in the eye when bending down cutting back one of the plants. Everyone needs to be mindful that it can be dangerous when working in your garden and you need to take extra care even when doing simple tasks.

From back to front:

Whilst sorting out our back beds (well Susie did all the work whilst I watched on from our decking because of my poorly knees) we took the opportunity to move our Aster plant from the back garden bed into the front grass bank bed. Where we hope it will make a nice display this autumn.

The Robin that lives in our garden was a constant companion while Susie and I worked in our garden…

AND - Darkness fell over all of the land:

Friday 20th March: At 9.36 am we had a partial solar eclipse of the sun. In Norfolk we saw about an 80% covering of the suns surface which lasted only a few moments but all went quite and darkness descended over the land.

Out came the shorts:

The puppies and I decided at 10 am that as it was a sunny morning we would go up the garden for a sit on the patio and have a coffee (you should always make time for a coffee). At 11 am as it was so nice I decided to go indoors and change into some shorts. It was great to feel the sun on my legs.

On went the sunglasses:

As the sun was so bright I also put on my sunglasses for the first time this year. We stayed in the garden until 4.30 pm and the temperature reached 12 °C. The puppies played on the lawn while the robin sang us a song from the silver birch tree, the daffodils and primroses are in full flower now whilst the snowdrops are gradually fading away. It truly felt that at last spring had sprung…

The final countdown:

I had a letter from the QE2 hospital in Kings Lynn asking me to attend the West Dereham Ward next Monday 23rd March at 10.30 am for a pre-admission and aftercare consultation and again on Wednesday 25th March at 9 am at the physiotherapy gym so a therapy and discharge plan can be agreed. As these are both part of the pre-assessment process prior to going in for my knee surgery I guess that it will not be long before I am called in for my operation. This is great news because my knees are getting more painful every day and I am finding it more and more difficult to walk with every passing day.

Getting my brushes out:

I decided to spend some of the time waiting for my appointments by sitting at our dining room table and doing the following watercolour painting:

My painting is called "Sailing off Skiathos" and reminds me of happy days spent watching the boats sail by while laying in the sea off Troulos Bay beach…

It's raining again!

It rained all day Tuesday and the puppies and I were unable to go out into the garden:

Poppy and Charlie had to shelter in the carport for most of the day…

Stop press news:

On Tuesday I also heard from the hospital that I will be admitted for my total left knee replacement operation at 7.30 am on Wednesday 1st April. Good news and so soon I hope that all the pain I have had over the years will come to an end. Here's hopping! So next week I will be going to the hospital twice Monday and Wednesday and then Susie and Ginny will be going up to stay with Lou, Gerard and Olivia on Thursday and attend Pete's funeral in Sheffield on Friday.

House front in 2019…

Brown bin…

Back to work:

Susie went back to work today (Tuesday) but she will come with me on Monday and then of course go up to Sheffield (Thursday and Friday) before taking the next two weeks off work so she can look after the puppies whilst I am in hospital (Wednesday 1st – Friday 3rd April) and also to look after me when I get home from hospital…

Busy last few days:

Saturday 21st – Tuesday 31st March: The last few days have been very busy with all the visits to hospital and Sheffield so I spent what spare time I had in doing a few watercolours to while away the time before the big day of April 1st.

Lions Kings of the African plain

Polperro harbour Cornwall…

April 2015

ALL Fools Day but for me it is the day of my knee operation:

Wednesday the 1st of April: Which is traditionally the day for playing practical jokes on friends and family but for me this year it is the day when I go into the Queen Elizabeth II hospital at 7.30 am for my total left knee replacement surgery:

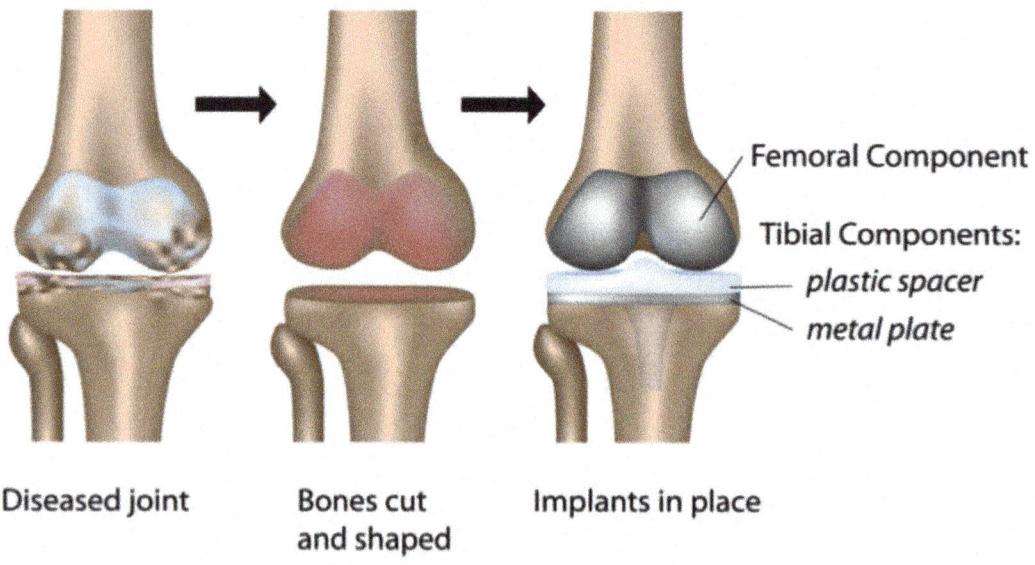

My surgeon Mr. Jeffery's has told me that if all goes well I should be home again on Friday 3rd April and that it will take three or more months for me to recover from the surgery! So please keep your fingers crossed that all goes well although it will mean that Susie will have to do all of this year's seed, tubers, bulb and plant planting and everything else the garden needs by way of maintenance for the next few months. Hopefully when I get home and feeling up to it I will let you know how it went…

The first cut is the deepest (Baby I Know!):

Wednesday 1st April: We left home at 6.50 am and arrived at the Q.E. II hospital at 7.15 am and made our way to the Marham ward for my pre-surgery preparation.

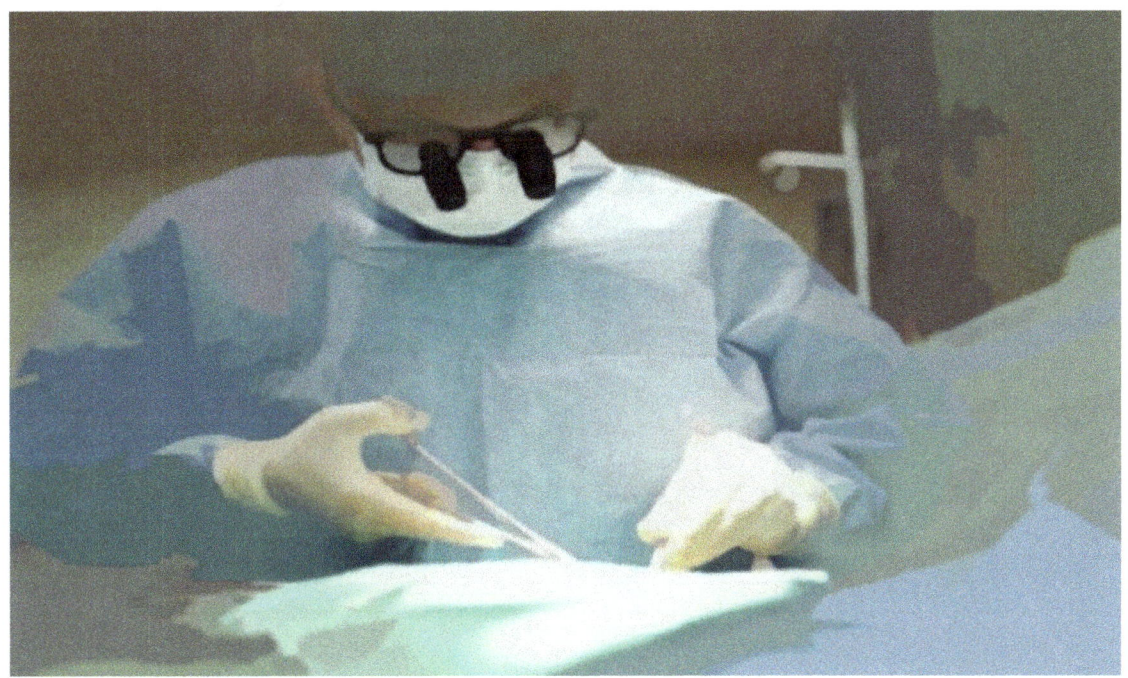

I was first on the list and went down to the operating theatre number 3 at 8.10 am. Susie gave me a good luck kiss at the door. There were six people in the operating theatre plus Mr Jeffery's my surgeon. I had an injection in my back ready for my surgery. This failed to work so they tried an injection into my thigh which also failed to numb my leg. Mr Jeffery's then discussed with me the options left open to us and we agreed on a general anaesthetic.

I woke up in the recovery room some five hours later in pain but I was pleased to see that my left foot was still there and I could move it! I was very well looked after by the surgical team and was taken up to the Elm ward when they were happy that I was out of immediate danger and my pain had subsided. I do not remember too much of the rest of Wednesday but I recall that the surgeon, houseman and other members of the surgical team all came and saw me and Mr. Jeffery's told me that all had gone very well…

Notes from a Hospital bed:

Wednesday 1st April – Saturday 4th April: For the next three nights I settled into the routine of hospital life that started at 5.20 am and after meals, pain relief, physiotherapy, nursing, doctor and surgeon visits it was time for Susie to come and visit me (which she did every day) before settling back down for the night at 10 pm.

The BIG Day:

Saturday 4th April: My physiotherapist Mike came this morning and made sure that my knee could bend to 70 degrees and that I could go up and down stairs safely then he and my surgeon Mr. Jeffery's signed my hospital release and told me I could go home today. I thanked the ward sister Rebecca and her nursing team for all their great care and then phoned Susie and told her the good news.

The great escape:

Susie came and collected me at 1 pm. She had not only cleaned the house from top to bottom, installed my new reclining chair in the lounge but had also spent a lot of time training the dogs to be calm and gentle around me…

Back in the swing:

Well not a swing as such but after getting down the stairs safely this morning it was armed with my elbow crutches and out into our beloved garden. I sat on the patio with Susie and the dogs in the warm April sun glad to be home.

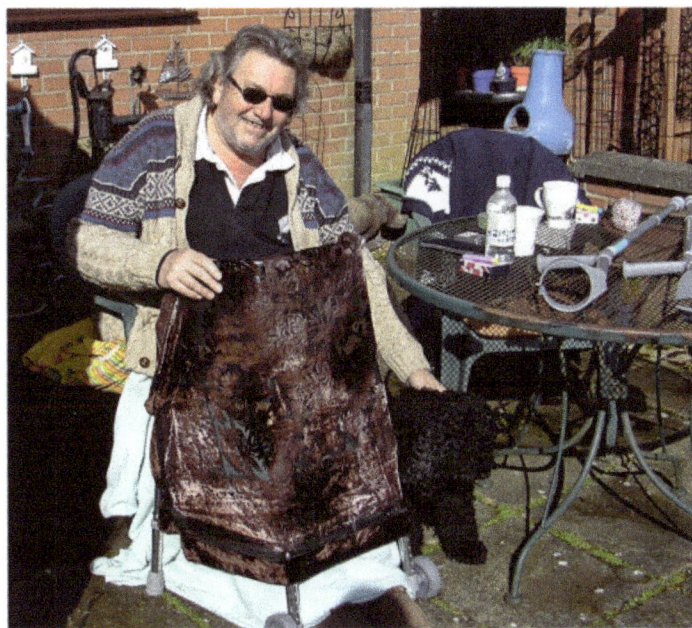

The dogs and Alan enjoying the sun…

Good boy (Charlie) and girls (Susie and Poppy):

Susie has taken two weeks holiday from work to be able to help me recover from my surgery. This has proved to be vital as I would not have been able to cope on my own initially because of my lack of mobility. While I was in hospital Susie had obviously spent a lot of time training the dogs not to jump up at me and had also managed to turn my walking frame (supplied by the QE2) into a piece of defensive art. So my return home went very well thanks to all her efforts to protect me.

Hard work:

Not me you understand but Susie. She has not only looked after me, made great meals, taken the dogs on long walks in the Warren but has also found the time to do a lot of gardening. What would I do without this girl?…

Action girl:

Monday 6th April – Sunday 12th April: Susie my all action girl worked hard in the garden while I sat on the patio with the dogs and completed the following:

- Hoed, sowed wild flower seed and top dressed the silver birch bed and patio bed.
- Brought more garden ornaments out of our shed and carefully positioned then around the garden.
- Gave the lawn its first cut of the garden season and it looked great afterwards.
- Started to harden off the cuttings outside from the greenhouse and sun lounge.
- Planted the perennials that we have over wintered in the greenhouse into patio pots.

On Thursday 9th April the swallows at last arrived in the sky above our garden once more. Oh happy days…

Nearly there!

Monday 13th April – Friday 17th April: Susie continued to work hard in our garden this week and completed the following:

- Applied blood, fish and bone fertiliser to all of our back garden flower beds.
- Emptied the greenhouse of all of the flower pots of plants that we have over wintered in there and put them on the patio.
- Took down the bubble wrap that we use in the greenhouse to help keep it frost free over winter.
- Gave the lawn its second cut of the year with the lawn mower and put the cuttings into our recycling bin.

Alan in Shades…

While Susie was doing all of the above I was able to sit on the patio and enjoy the April sunshine…

Being prepared:

Saturday 18th April – Sunday 19th April: This morning Susie went off to the Downham Country Store to get some new wall basket liners, three bags of compost and some radish, spring onion and beetroot seeds. While there she also got 37 trailing plants for our cages, hanging and wall baskets:

- 10 white trailing lobelia.
- 10 blue trailing lobelia.
- 10 mixed colours petunias
- 3 mixed million bells.
- 4 mixed trailing petunias.

Susie, on Sunday, put the liners and compost into the cages, wall and hanging baskets before planting her newly acquired plants into them. She will keep them in the greenhouse for the next few weeks to protect them from any late frosts and open the door each day to let fresh air in to help harden them off before closing the door up again at night. We will put them in their final flowering positions in about three weeks' time.

While Susie was doing all of the above I was able to sit on the patio and enjoy the April sunshine and watch the ever increasing numbers of swallows and house martins swooping in the sky above our garden…

On my own (not really):

Monday 20th April – Thursday 23rd April: Now that Susie has returned to work and left me alone all day with the dogs the weather has changed from warm and sunny to cold and wet. Just our luck however, in my current state I cannot do any gardening anyway and will be unlikely to be able to for some weeks to come. So with this in mind I asked Susie to set up her computer onto our dining room table so I could complete this book.

In the next few pages I will share with you some of my gardening tips that have worked for me and I leave you with some words from the Rolling Stones who say it best:

It's all over now…

Gardening tips and ideas:

Friday April 24th: As we come to the end of another year together I thought that as I have often been given good gardening advice either from friends, family, books or radio/TV programmes and also learnt from my own experiences in the our garden of what has worked for me and what doesn't.

Over the years that I have been gardening I have gleaned some very useful gardening tips. The following tips and ideas have worked for me and I use them in our garden. I offer them to the reader for their consideration…

Tips:

- Using lengths of galvanised wire to secure pre-drilled wooden fencing panels by winding it around fence panels and posts.
- Prune back to about 50 cm your early flowering clematis on the 14th February.
- Use horticultural grit to top dress your potted up pots to help retain water and suppress weeds.
- Nip out the top shoots of dahlias when they have put up at least four leaf buds to encourage a stronger plant and stimulate the plant to produce more flowers.
- Enhance old terra cotta pots by painting them with colourful small pots of masonry paint.
- Use a handful of Blood. Fish and Bone fertilizer in the planting hole when you put new plants in the garden or pots etc.
- Use bubble wrap to insulate your greenhouse in the autumn and winter months.
- Use something like an old bed sheet on the ground under any plants, shrubs or hedging to catch the off cuts when cutting back. This makes it far easier when tiding up afterwards.
- Line your hanging baskets and wall mounted baskets with cut down old compost bags to better retain water but remember to put a few holes in the plastic before filling it with soil and plants to allow drainage.
- Use "Magic Powder" hormone powder when taking cuttings to promote rooting.
- Use a light weight stripped plastic door curtain on the inside of your greenhouse door to give added shading whilst acting as a barrier to birds and other flying insects.

More tips to follow…

More tips:

- Use paper mushroom bags to store your dahlia and other tubers that require lifting before the frosts come and store them over winter indoors.
- Use a battery operated hedge trimmer or garden shears to reduce the height of such plants as salvias, lavender, bushes and hedges (don't forget to put your old bed sheet down before starting to catch the off cuts).
- Use a car touch up spray can of car paint to re-fresh your metal garden ornaments (use your sheet above to protect other things around the item being sprayed and don't do it on a windy day!).
- Use old redundant garden equipment as flower display opportunities e.g. wheelbarrow, Chiminea, watering can etc. (you can even spray them up as above).
- Collect any fallen leaves in autumn and put them in an old compost bag (a few holes in the bottom for drainage) and store behind your shed/garage for a year or so and hey presto you have your own free leaf mould.
- Dogs can make useful dead heading machines but be aware they may dig and make a mess of you garden and/or lawn so like us invest in dog proof fencing to keep them out of areas you do not want them in!
- DO NOT cut your Leylandi hedge to within an inch of its life! Use evergreen clematis to cover over any mistakes.
- Take extra care when undertaking any garden tasks even when you are just stepping out of your greenhouse!
- Use the magic fairy (washing up liquid) to stop condensation on your greenhouse glazing.

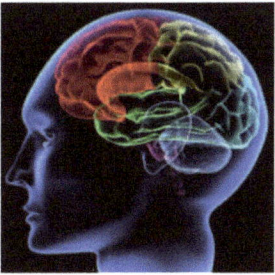

Remember to always engage your brain before undertaking any of the above tasks or anything else you do and now we will look at how to make free plants…

Tips on Taking Cuttings:

Penstemon:

- In mid-spring, check plants for new shoots at the base or along the stems

- Where shoots are growing from the base, cut out all the old stems close to the bottom

- Penstemon with few or no shoots growing from ground level should only have their stems shortened, making the cuts just above the lowest set of healthy leaves

- Once a plant has been pruned, remove weeds and other encroaching plants…

Tips on Propagation:

Because many penstemon's are not reliably hardy, a hard winter can result in serious losses. It is therefore advisable to propagate some fresh stock each year in late summer and keep it in frost-free conditions until the following year. Cuttings are the best method when propagating a named cultivar, as these do not come reliably true from seed. However, seed, division and layering can also be used. See the notes below for more on these techniques.

How to take Softwood cuttings:

This is the best method to produce plants true to the parent. Softwood cuttings can be taken any time during the growing season – those taken early in the year require bottom heat. The more vigorous cultivars, such as Penstemon 'Alice Hindley' and P. 'Schoenholzeri' can be taken early in the year (for planting out in early summer) and usually grow rapidly enough to give a flower display by late summer…

Method used to take softwood cuttings:

- Take non-flowering tip cuttings of about 10-12.5 cm (4-5 in) long and trim with a sharp knife to just below a leaf node
- Gently remove the bottom two leaves and trim the top and side leaves by up to one-third to reduce leaf surface area and, in turn, moisture loss
- Dip the cut ends in hormone rooting powder and insert in a 50:50 mixture of compost and perlite
- Up to five cuttings can be inserted into a 9 cm (3.5 in) pot, or modular trays can be used for larger quantities
- After rooting, they can be left undisturbed over winter or individually potted on

Rooted cuttings of penstemon's need frost-free conditions during the winter, but can otherwise be grown with little or no warmth and should be kept as cool as practical, with good ventilation whenever possible...

Growing Penstemon's from seed:

Penstemon's are easily propagated from seed sown in early spring in heated conditions and planted out in early summer. However they are unlikely to come true to the parent plant.

Penstemon grown from seed and the lone hedgehog…

When to take Clematis cuttings:

Start in late spring and your cuttings will root within a few weeks and be ready to plant out in the summer.

Taking Clematis cuttings – What to do:

- For best results select a healthy shoot from the current season's growth about 90 cm (3 ft) long and remove from the plant by cutting above a leaf joint with secateurs, taking care not to damage any buds.
- Place shoots in a plastic bag moistened with water - this will help to keep the material fresh and prevent wilting…

Taking Clematis cuttings – What to do:

- To make cuttings, take your shoots and divide them with a knife, cutting immediately above a leaf joint and then severing again, 5 cm (2 in) beneath it. Avoid using the very tips of the shoot as they're likely to be too soft.
- Remove one of the leaves from each cutting to help reduce moisture loss and allow more to be planted into the same pot, avoiding overcrowding.
- Dip the base of the cutting into hormone rooting powder and shake off any excess.
- Fill a 7.5 cm (3 in) pot with compost (a mix of 50 per cent cuttings compost and 50 per cent horticultural grit), level and firm.
- Insert several cuttings around the edge of the pot, pushing in until the leaf joint is level with the surface.
- Water and either place the pot in a windowsill propagator or cover with a clear polythene bag, held secure with an elastic band. This will help to speed up rooting…

Aftercare for Clematis cuttings:

- Keep compost moist and cuttings should root within several weeks.
- A good indicator is when the leaves appear to perk up. You can check further by looking for roots emerging through the drainage holes at the bottom of the pot.
- Once rooted, remove the pot and gently split the root ball apart, keeping as much compost around the roots as possible.
- Put each cutting into its own pot, making sure it is planted at the same level as before.
- Water and put in a cool place, such as a cold frame and plant into your garden during spring.

It is also possible to propagate clematis by layering and species clematis can be grown from seed...

More tips on soft wood cuttings:

These propagation methods are suitable for tender perennials such as bidens, gazania, heliotrope, marguerites and verbena. All root quickly and easily, as do other frost tender plants including fuchsias, pelargoniums, penstemon's and salvias.

Although you can lift or mulch such plants in autumn, cutting them back and keeping them under glass over winter, they can become woody and are best replaced with young plants raised from cuttings. Winter is too late to take cuttings so you must plan ahead before the season is out.

- Take softwood cuttings of pelargoniums, petunias, bidens, fuchsias and penstemons in spring and summer from new growth when the swallows are in the sky
- Semi-ripe cuttings of penstemon's, salvias, argyranthemum, verbena and heliotrope can be taken from summer to early autumn when the base of the cutting is hardening and the non-flowering tip is still soft…

Tips on How to take Cuttings:

Most tender perennials propagate easily from cuttings. There are two methods that are particularly useful: semi-ripe cuttings and softwood cuttings.

Most cuttings taken in spring will be flowering in their first summer. Those taken in late summer and will need over wintering under glass and will be ready to harden off during May. One of the keys to over wintering rooted cuttings under glass is to keep them on the dry side in bright frost-free conditions of around 7°C (45°F).

Your cuttings can make a real difference in your beds and pots next summer and really help you fill your garden with colour…

Tips on How to Make more plants for your garden:

Our garden Robin is a constant visitor to our garden and often just stands there and watch me as I take my cuttings from plants close by or when I layer or make a division of plants in the beds.

Making new plants by Layering: Layering is a means of plant propagation in which a portion of an aerial stem grows roots while still attached to the parent plant and then detaches as an independent plant.

Layering has evolved as a common means of vegetative propagation of numerous species in natural environments.

Making new plants by Division: Division, in horticulture and gardening, is a method of asexual plant propagation, where the plant (usually an herbaceous perennial) is broken up into two or more parts. Both the root and crown of each part is kept intact. These can then be re-planted into the garden…

Last few Days:

All our hard work in our garden this year has been so worthwhile and yes I am really looking forward to doing it all again starting next week (honest). We hope to book another holiday to Troulos Bay Hotel Skiathos soon as a reward for us both for all our hard work especially Susie while I recovered from my knee surgery. **YES...**

The Key: In conclusion the key to a happy retirement to the garden upon reflection is to identify areas that can be improved in your garden and plan projects to achieve them. This will help keep you both fit and focused. Some of the projects that we have completed so far are:

- Made an alpine display in our old unused wheelbarrow
- Put a new bed into the grass in the front garden bank
- Provided Susie with a designated herb growing area (table top)
- Re-located our arbour from top patio down nearer the house
- Bought and erected a greenhouse on the back garden top patio
- Put a new bed in the back garden lawn to grow roses
- Extended the patio where the greenhouse was erected
- Bought seeds and plug plants to grow on to populate pots/beds
- Constructed wooden trough for cut flowers in the greenhouse
- Constructed wooden decking patio behind the new rose bed
- Emptied/revamped/replanted bed in front of the house patio
- Re-treated front fences, shed and seats with wood preserver

What to do next?

I think that it is time to move onto some fresh writing challenges so later this year I will start on two new books the first one will be based on **our paradise Greek island of Skiathos and the second will feature the county of my birth Norfolk...**

Parting is such sweet sorrow:

Friday 24th April 2015: Well it's time for us to part (always a sad time) as we reach the end of another year in the journey through a **"Year in the life of our garden".**

Retirement is often an opportunity to do the things that you have always wanted to do. In my case this has been so true. **The act of "Retiring to our garden"** has been a thing of great joy and satisfaction to me and I would recommend it to everyone.

Remember you also need a supportive and hardworking partner to make your garden bloom. I am lucky I have Susie. I look forward very much too the coming year in our garden so goodbye for now and until next time…

Happy Gardening

Best Wishes from Alan and Susie xxx.

They think it's all over…**IT IS NOW!**

The Prologue

Norwich…

Monday 1st June 2015: As I finished reading the first proof draft of this book I decided to add in this prologue to give my readers updates on some of the key issues still ongoing as we finished our journey through a year in our garden in April. We will have a look at how Norwich City football club finished the current session, how my recovery from surgery has gone and have a final look at our garden first in June 2016 and again bringing it right up to date on the 26th June 2019…

The Prologue

The all clear: Monday 18th May 2015: Susie and I went to the Queen Elizabeth hospital in Kings Lynn today to see Mr Jeffery's my orthopaedic surgeon who undertook my total knee replacement operation on April 1st. After having an x-ray we went in to see him and after reviewing the x-ray and examining my knee he pronounced that he was happy with it and I should make a full recovery in the next month or so. Thursday 21st May 2015 I attended my weekly physiotherapy knee class at the hospital and after achieving a 95 degree bend to my left knee I was told that I did not need to attend classes anymore. This was great news and as I complete my recovery from the surgery I must thank my physiotherapists Mike, Leon and Claire as well as Elm Ward sister Rebecca and her nursing team for all their great care and last but not least Mr. Jeffery's and his surgical team.

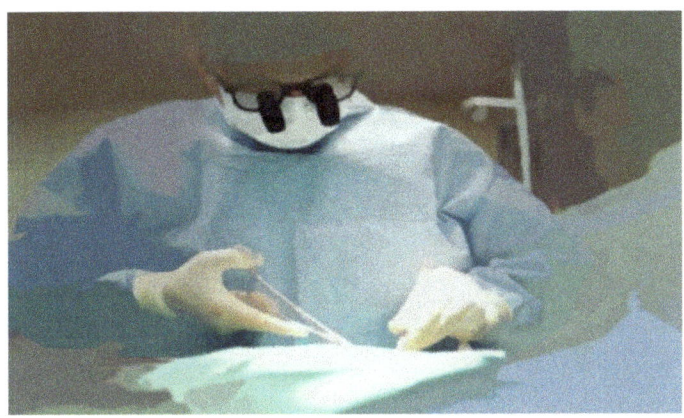

In September 2016 I returned to hospital to have my right knee replacement surgery. It was performed once again by Mr. Jeffery and again my recovery was good.

In June 2019 I am not pain free but much improved and hope to hobble around on my false knees for any more years to come...

The Prologue

The last chance: Norwich City Football Club finished the current season in third place in the championship which meant they had to go into the playoffs in an attempt to gain promotion to the Premier league next season. In the semi-final they had to play local revels Ipswich Town first away at Portman Road where they drew 1 – 1 and then it was back to Carrow Road where they won 3 – 1 to qualify for the final at Wembley Stadium on Monday 25th May. **We're going to Wembley:** The Canaries played very well in the match and beat Middlesbrough 2 – 0 and will therefore be in the Premier League next season.
Oh happy days and deep joy.

Although we were relegated the very next season I am proud to announce that we gained promotion back to the Premier League once more in the 2018 - 2019 season. So once more we will be playing with the big boys come August 2019.

WE ARE Going UP, UP, UP - AGAIN…

The Prologue

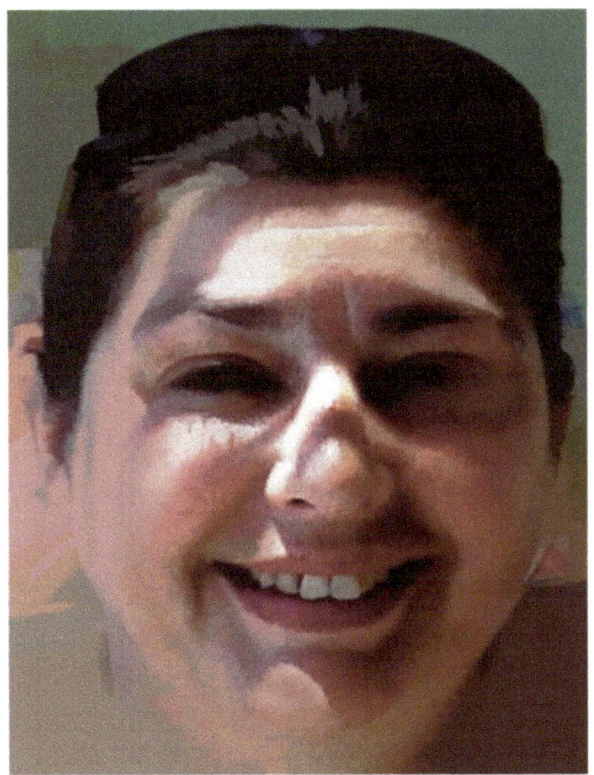

My Shinning STAR: Susie has been my nurse, companion, coach and support throughout my recovery from the major surgery on my knee. As well as all this extra work she has looked after our dogs, kept our garden tidy and planted all this seasons plants into beds, baskets and pots whilst working full time. She has done this willingly and with a smile on her face and she really is my star and I would have been lost without her..

The Prologue

Finally: To end this prologue we will have a look at some recent pictures of our dogs and our garden on the 26th June 2016 up to 1st July 2019.

Above we see Poppy warning Charlie off and poor old Charlie standing on his own wondering what all the fuss was about after having a close shave!…

The Prologue

Poppy and the Patio in our garden…

The Prologue

Poppy in the garden…

The Prologue

Flowers in our garden…

The Prologue

Flowers in our garden…

The Prologue

Ginny and Bertie with foxgloves…

The Prologue

Poppy and Charlie in the long grass…

The Prologue

Thistle and foxgloves in our local dog walking woods…

The Prologue

Our garden patio…

The Prologue

Flowers in our garden…

The Prologue

The wishing well and a poppy in our garden…

The Prologue

New poppy wall ornament, Susie, Poppy and patio table…

The Prologue

Charlie and Poppy relaxing in our garden…

The Prologue

Our friends Karl and Anna at Troulos Bay in June 2016 and our late friend Roy relaxing on holiday in 2017 (he died in November 2018)…

The Prologue

Our friend Corri in her garden and our friends Andy and Lynn on Troulos Bay beach on Skiathos…

The Prologue

Pictures of our garden…

The Prologue

Charlie and Poppy relaxing in our garden…

The Prologue

The decking and patio in our garden…

The Prologue

Our re-designed front garden bank completed in May 2019…

The Prologue: Time to say goodbye to our garden.

Finally it's goodbye from me and its goodbye from Susie – Happy Gardening…

Acknowledgement

In addition to all of the retailers (materials and plants), family, friends and Skiathans mentioned or illustrated in this book who have enriched my life immeasurably, I wish to express my gratitude to Rainbow Publications UK for giving me the opportunity for my words to be read once more. Finally I wish to thank my wife Susie for her love and support in all that I do.

Copyright © 2019 Alan R. Massen

and to you my reader I give you a special

Thank You